PRICE WATERHOUSE PERSONAL TAX ADVISOR

The Canadian Price Waterhouse Personal Tax Advisor

A Seal Book/February 1989

Design: Don Fernley
Editing: The Editorial Centre
Typesetting: Compeer Typographic Services

Printed and bound in Canada by Gagne

This publication is intended to offer guidance on personal tax matters. It is sold with the understanding that the author and publisher are not herein engaged in rendering legal, tax, or other professional services. This book should not be used as a substitute for professional advice.

Canadian Cataloguing in Publication Data

Birch, Richard, 1945–
The Canadian Price Waterhouse personal tax advisor

ISBN 0-7704-2290-X

1. Income tax — Canada. 2. Tax returns — Canada.
I. Price Waterhouse (Firm). II. Title.

HJ4661.B57 1989 343.7105'2044 C88-094932-5

Contents

Introduction

Few of us resent paying tax—we would just like to pay a little less.

And many Canadians could easily pay less. All it takes is a little planning. But why should you bother if it only means a few dollars? This may be true in some cases, but in most, the savings could amount to a few hundred dollars, or even a few thousand—each and every year. It all depends on your personal finances.

But one thing is sure—each dollar that does not go into the Government's tax coffers goes directly into your pocket. You may not have quick and easy access to those funds if, for example, they go into your RRSP. Still, they are your dollars, not the taxman's.

Tax planning focuses on minimizing your tax bill, both in the short and longer term. You can do this in two ways—by achieving an absolute reduction in tax payable, and by postponing the payment of tax to future years—that is, deferring tax.

Putting an effective personal tax strategy into operation will make demands on your cash flow. For example, in order to defer tax, it may be necessary to delay receiving some income, or you may have to set aside money that will then not be available for day-to-day spending. As a result, your tax strategy must take into account your anticipated cash requirements; otherwise, you could be left short of funds.

Tax planning is one of the key aspects of personal financial planning, which has as its primary goal long-term security. If you have implemented an effective personal tax strategy, it probably means that your financial affairs are in good order and will stay that way. You will not be looking forward to any surprises, except the pleasant kind, and you will be in a position to achieve your personal goals.

The time to begin tax planning is now. But you should continue to develop your overall tax strategy throughout the year. Opportunities often present themselves when you least expect them, not only at the end of the year. And April 30 is too late to do anything about last year's taxes.

The place to begin is your most recent tax return. Review your sources of income, deductions and tax credits. You might also take a quick trip through the guide that came with your return. Next, settle down with this book for an evening or two, and at the same time review your, and your family's, complete financial situation. Make a note of the planning opportunities that could definitely apply and any that might apply if you undertake any of the financial transactions you have been contemplating. Finally, talk to your professional tax advisor. You can put many of the ideas into action yourself, but you may need professional help with others. A number of the ideas may need the expertise of a professional to determine how your personal financial situation could be affected if you implement the idea.

The sentence "Professional advice is a must" crops up more than once in the book. The reason is simple. Tax law is extremely complex and much of it is open to interpretation. You will need the opinion of a professional to draw the line between aggressive, legitimate tax planning and going overboard into the realm of tax evasion. As well, the law is constantly being changed. Your professional advisor can keep you up-to-date and let you know about new developments and new opportunities.

This book is based on the federal and provincial law in effect at the end of September 1988, on the pension reform proposals released as draft legislation in March 1988 and modified in August 1988 and on various statements made by the Government relating to tax to the end of September 1988. We cannot stress too strongly that you review your personal tax strategy with your professional tax advisor to ensure that it properly and accurately reflects both your actual position and any subsequent changes to the law described in this book that may affect it.

Disclaimer

The tax-planning comments and advice outlined in this book are intended as a general guide only. This book is sold with the understanding that, while every reasonable care has been taken to ensure the accuracy of the text, neither the publisher nor the authors can be held responsible for any omissions or errors. Because tax planning must be related to individual circumstances, the publisher and the authors cannot be liable for losses or risks with respect to the implementation of specific tax-planning concepts. In this connection, we would point out that changes in the interpretation of the law or in the Department of National Revenue's administrative policy may have a material impact on recommendations made by the authors. This book should not be used as a substitute for professional advice, and if you have any questions about your tax-planning program, you should consult with a professional advisor.

1

The Canadian Tax System and How You Fit In

It's true. Tax reform has affected almost every Canadian taxpayer. Most employees saw their take-home pay increase in the middle of 1988 because less tax was being withheld from their wages. And all of us must now confront a brand new tax return—just when we were becoming at least a little bit familiar with the old one.

But for all the talk we've heard about tax reform over the past two years, the fundamentals of the tax system remain unchanged.

Who's Taxed and What's Taxable

Residents of Canada are taxed on their world-wide income. Generally, you are considered to be a Canadian resident if you live here most of the year, although there are a number of exceptions. For example, you may be posted to another country for up to two years and retain Canadian residency for tax purposes. There is no statutory definition of Canadian residency, so each case is determined according to the specific facts and circumstances.

If you are a non-resident, but you retain your Canadian citizenship, there is no obligation, in most cases, to file a Canadian tax return, even though you might be receiving, perhaps, pension or investment income from Canada. A return must be filed if a non-resident is earning employment or business income in Canada, or realizes a capital gain on the disposition of taxable Canadian property.

Many retired Canadians live half the year in Canada and half in warmer climes, often in the southern United States. If you are in this situation and there is any doubt about your residency, you probably should take steps to establish it in one country or the other, assuming you have a choice. It's often not an easy matter to choose between two countries, so you should get professional help. There are dozens of things to consider, your tax liability being one of them but perhaps not the most important. Don't forget the Canada-United States tax treaty. One of its purposes is to eliminate double taxation in situations just like yours. In fact, it, and other tax treaties, contain tie-breaker rules that provide relief to individuals who find themselves resident in more than one country.

Most forms of income are taxable, including employment, investment and business incomes. But there are several notable exceptions, such as gifts and inheritances. Most types of insurance settlements and, in many circumstances, sums awarded by the courts are also not taxed. For some unfathomable reason, those lucky enough to win a lottery also win a tax exemption for their prize.

You can deduct certain outlays incurred to earn your income on your tax return. Union dues, or travelling expenses if you are in sales, are deductible if you earn employment income. You can also deduct interest expense incurred to earn investment income. As well, you can claim a variety of credits against federal and provincial tax payable.

The Government uses the tax system to finance the business of running the country, and also to pursue various economic and social goals. For example, deductions are allowed for pension and Registered Retirement Savings Plan (RRSP) contributions to encourage taxpayers to save for their retirement years. Tax credits are given to provide relief from the hardship of unusual medical expenses, to promote donations to charities and to reduce the tax burden of lower-income Canadians and the elderly. And in the interest of fair play, if you have paid foreign taxes on your income, credit against Canadian tax owing is generally allowed.

Don't forget that foreign income must be reported in your income tax return. However, to reduce the amount to be included in your return, you may deduct appropriate expenses from the income. If you are reporting foreign investment or business income, such as rental income from your Florida condominium, you may want to have a professional review your sideline business this year to ensure that you are claiming all the appropriate expenses and that your tax returns are filled out properly.

Doing It Yourself

Canada's tax system is *self-assessing*, which simply means that the onus is on you to file a complete and correct tax return each year by the April 30 deadline. You must use the appropriate form, called a T-1, which is supplied by the Government. Depending on the complexity of your return, you might be required to use one or more of several dozen other Government-prescribed or approved forms.

On the T-1, you will determine your total federal and provincial tax liability, and reconcile this with the tax that has been withheld from your income during the year (reported on your T-4s or T-5s) or that you have paid by quarterly instalments (summarized for you periodically by Revenue Canada).

You must file a tax return if:

☐ Your income is large enough to attract tax after claiming deductions and tax credits,

☐ You must make Canada Pension Plan contributions or
☐ You have sold an asset (called a capital property) on which either a capital gain or loss has been realized.

As well, you must file a return to collect a tax refund or refundable tax credits. Those who received an advance payment on their refundable child tax credit must also file a return. All tax filers are required to have a social insurance number.

Remember that even though your employer may not withhold enough tax from your paycheques during the year, you are still liable for all tax owing. The Canadian tax contract is between you and the Government, not between you and the company for which you work. Employers only act as tax-collecting agents for the Government. You owe the difference between the amount withheld and the amount you determine as your tax liability for the year. Look on the bright side. Throughout the year, you, not the Government, had the use of the money you now owe as tax. You might want to look on it as an interest-free loan from Revenue Canada. You may want to submit a new TD-1 form (the form you use to let your employer know about your entitlement to personal tax credits) so that your employer will be able to correctly determine how much tax to withhold from your wages.

TAX TIP It pays to file your tax return on or before the April 30 deadline, even if you owe tax but do not have the cash to pay at that time. You will avoid the late-filing penalty (see Chapter 16), which can be harsh if you are a second-time offender. If you have not received information slips, such as T-4s or T-5s, file your return with a note explaining your problem.

You've heard the expression "ignorance of the law is no excuse". It applies to tax law also. A variety of penalties apply if you do not observe the tax law. They tend to be more severe if it can be established that you willingly or knowingly flaunt the law. Revenue Canada Taxation interprets and administers this law, and is also responsible for collecting the tax.

Fortunately, the Government has devoted considerable resources to helping you comply with its rules. The guide that accompanies your tax return contains enough information to take the average wage earner successfully through the preparation of his or her own return. Last year's guide was particularly helpful, providing a variety of useful tips. If you had followed only a few of these, you might have actually reduced your tax bill, perhaps by several hundred dollars. Who says the taxman doesn't have a heart?

This book will also help you understand your tax return and make your trek through it this spring a little easier. But as noted in the introduction, the primary purpose is to help you put together a comprehensive tax plan to reduce the amount of tax you pay this year and in the years to come.

2

The New Rate Structure and Tax Credit System

This tax year, 1988, Canadians will have their first close encounter with our "reformed" tax system. On your tax return, which looks quite different from last year's, you will have the dubious pleasure of calculating your tax liability using the new three-bracket rate structure, and you will be able to pick your way through at least twenty tax credits, a baker's dozen of which are brand new.

How you are affected by the new system depends on the complexity of your personal finances. Many employees earning an "average" income won't notice any difference except for a slightly lower tax bill. Nevertheless, you should plan on spending an extra evening or two with the new tax form and its accompanying guide.

You may not fare as well if your finances are more complicated and your financial decisions are, at least to some extent, "tax-motivated". You will not necessarily have more cash in your pocket at year end just because tax rates are generally declining.

Know Thy Tax Bracket

The new three-tiered tax rate structure contributes, at least to some extent, to tax simplification. (Few other tax reform measures do.) It also may simplify many financial decisions that hinge on potential tax liability. Most conspicuously, the structure clearly defines who the Government considers to be upper, middle or lower income. As many of us have suspected, the difference between upper and middle income has become blurred.

The federal rates are 17%, 26% and 29%, down from the high of 34% last year. But don't forget that the provinces want their share—anywhere from 43% to 60% of the federal slice. Throughout this book, we will use the percentages shown below for combined federal and provincial tax rates, based on the assumption that the average provincial tax rate is in the neighbourhood of 55% of the federal rate and that surtaxes are probably here to stay.

Taxable Income	*Federal Tax Rate**	*Combined Federal and Provincial Tax Rate**
First $27,500	17%	26%
Next $27,500	26%	40%
Above $55,000	29%	45%

*These rates do not reflect the 3% federal surtax or any provincial surtaxes.

The right-hand column shows your marginal tax rate, which is simply the rate of tax that you pay on your last dollar earned in the year. It's also the rate at which you save tax if you manage to reduce your income. For example, if you are in the middle 40% tax bracket and you receive a $1,000 bonus in December, $400 of tax will be payable on the bonus at your marginal rate of 40%. On the other hand, suppose that you contribute $1,000 to an RRSP (see Chapter 5). You get to deduct $1,000 from your income, producing a tax saving of $400 at your marginal tax rate of 40%.

Your marginal rate of tax is what you are concerned with when making investment or financial decisions that are to any degree tax-motivated. For example, tax shelters (only a few remain—see Chapter 12) are generally of interest only to persons in the top tax bracket because much of their benefit arises from tax savings. If you are saving $46 in tax for each $100 invested, the shelter will be more attractive than if you are only saving $26 in tax.

Your average or effective tax rate is calculated by dividing total tax paid by total income. For example, if your income is $40,000 and you pay tax of $8,000, your average tax rate is 20% ($8,000/$40,000). However, your marginal tax rate is 40% since your taxable income is between $27,500 and $55,000. Knowing your average tax rate is not particularly useful. While it tells you how much of your earnings you share with the Government, it does not actually help you make informed financial decisions. For example, you would be more likely to make the $1,000 RRSP contribution knowing that your tax saving will be $400 at your marginal rate of 40%, and not just $200 at your average tax rate of 20%.

Chances are good that your marginal rate of tax in 1988 and 1989 will be different from your marginal rate in 1987, perhaps by a significant degree. There are two reasons for this difference. The most obvious reason is the change in the rate structure.

The second reason is that taxable income in 1988 is not the same as taxable income in 1987. Because many of the deductions and exemptions were converted to tax credits, you now arrive at taxable income on your tax return much sooner than last year. For example, assume that your income was about $35,000 last year and it hasn't changed this year. Last year, with a variety of deductions and personal exemptions, your taxable income was about $20,000 and your marginal tax rate was about 35%. This year, you have only $4,000 in deductions, leaving you with a taxable income of

$31,000 ($35,000 minus $4,000) and a marginal tax rate of 40%.

What this means is that a $1,000 RRSP contribution produces a $50 larger tax saving this year ($400 versus $350 last year), but a $1,000 December bonus attracts an extra $50 in tax. Remember though, your overall tax burden in 1988 has probably declined, courtesy of the new system.

TAX TIP At certain income levels, it can pay to know your marginal tax rate. If your income in 1988 is in the $30,000 range and deductions bring your income down to the $27,500 threshold, your marginal tax rate is 26% for tax savings (transactions that lower your taxable income). However, your marginal tax rate is 40% for tax costs (that is, if you increase your taxable income above the $27,500 threshold).

Tax Credits—The Better Way

Tax credits are indeed a fairer way to provide tax reductions. Why? Because all taxpayers benefit to the same extent when claiming tax credits. With deductions, or exemptions, a person in the top tax bracket benefits more than someone in the lowest bracket. For example, if the basic tax credit for a single individual were instead a deductible exemption of $6,000, a person in the top bracket would get a tax saving of $2,700 (i.e., 45% of $6,000), while a person in the lowest bracket would save only $1,560 (26% of $6,000) in taxes. In 1988, every taxpayer is entitled to the same tax credit — $1,020 (federal) plus about $540 (provincial), for a total of $1,560. The person in the lowest bracket is no worse off with the tax credit, while taxpayers in the higher two brackets will not save as much tax. Table 1 summarizes the tax credits that replace the personal exemptions from last year.

Table 1
1988 Personal Tax Credits (Federal)

Basic personal	$1,020
Married	850
Spouse's exempt income	500
Dependent children*	
– under 18 at any time in the year	65**
– 19 or over and infirm	250
– 18 or over	Nil
Age 65 and over	550
Pension income (17% × eligible income)	170 (max.)

*Credits reduced by child's net income exceeding $2,500.
**$130 per child for 3rd and subsequent children.

The conversion to tax credits is accompanied by several other changes. First the bad news. The exemption for dependent children who are over eighteen at the end of the year is not replaced by a tax credit. Instead, parents may be able to gain access to the new tuition tax credit (see next chapter), which is transferable from the student to someone who is supporting him or her.

But the news is mostly good. A dependent spouse can still earn up to $500 and the married-status tax credit is not affected. As the spouse earns more income, the credit is reduced proportionately. However, it will not completely disappear until the spouse has a net income of at least $5,500, up from the $4,220 threshold in 1987. As well, the "tax penalty" that results if a spouse earns over $500 but not enough to be taxable has declined in 1988 because of the tax credit system.

Many people ask whether it is really worthwhile, from a tax point of view, for their spouse to take a part-time job. Our answer is the same year after year: "a buck is a buck, and an after-tax buck is an after-tax buck. They're both better than no bucks at all". Yes, for each $100 that your spouse earns in excess of $500, you are going to lose $26 worth of married status tax credit. But that also means that your family will be $74 better off ($100 minus $26). Which would you rather have—$74 or nothing?

The news gets better. The maximum tax saving that you will lose is about $1,320 (the combined federal and provincial married-status tax credit). However, your spouse can probably earn between $7,500 and $8,000 before he or she pays any tax, after taking into account the credit for Canada Pension Plan and Unemployment Insurance premiums, as well as any RRSP contributions. In other words, up to $8,000 of additional income will cost your family as little as $1,320 in increased taxes. You could be better off by almost $6,700. But if you are in the 40% tax bracket and you were to earn that extra $8,000, you would be looking at a $3,200 jump in your tax bill. You would be better off by only $4,800 ($8,000 minus $3,200).

One other advantage arises if your spouse is earning this income. Since the full $8,000 is now in your spouse's hands, any income he or she earns on this amount will be taxed at a lower rate than if you had earned it. It may even escape tax altogether if your spouse's income is less than $8,000 (see Chapter 13 on income splitting). This is the kind of longer-term tax planning that leads to hundreds of dollars of tax savings every year.

Of course, when both spouses work, expenses tend to increase to some extent. In a few cases, couples have actually discovered that they have less money available, even though both are now working. You may want to crunch a few numbers through the family budget just to make sure that the second income is going to be financially rewarding.

The oddly named "equivalent-to-married tax credit" is most commonly available to single parents supporting their children. However, it is also available to other unmarried or separated individuals who wholly support a person related to them by blood, marriage or adoption.

The tax credit, which is worth about $1,320 in 1988 for one dependant only, can be claimed by only one occupant of a self-contained dwelling. With the price of housing rising, it is becoming more and more common for single parents to share a rented house with a friend in exactly the same situation. Unfortunately, both cannot claim the equivalent-to-married tax credit. Since they share the house, there is only one dwelling and therefore only one person is entitled to claim the tax credit. The other person gets to claim the dependent tax credit, which is worth only about $100. If the two parties can't agree on who gets the equivalent-to-married tax credit, neither gets it.

Refundable Tax Credits

Only two of the twenty tax credits are refundable. Refundable means that you receive the tax credit in the form of a tax refund whether or not you owe any tax. Some commentators have called these tax credits a "negative income tax". The other eighteen credits can only be applied against tax owing.

To receive the refundable child tax credit or refundable sales tax credit, you must file a tax return. You must also have a social insurance number (SIN). Both credits are available only to lower-income persons – you must meet an income test. The child tax credit is available to the person who is eligible for Family Allowance payments. Details are included in your tax return. You can now receive an advance payment on the refundable child tax credit.

Forward Averaging—A System Whose Time Hadn't Come

According to the Government, forward averaging became pointless in 1988 when the new tax rate structure took effect. Some think the system was scrapped because it was complex and not being used by many taxpayers. Forward averaging was designed to help those whose income took a jump one year and would be taxed at unusually high rates. Those who qualified could include a certain portion of their earnings in income for tax purposes in a future year, when presumably it would be taxable at a lower rate. Unfortunately, when they elected to forward average, they immediately had to pay a special tax on this income at the highest rate and then receive credit for this tax when the amount forward averaged was eventually included in income. Those who have opted to use forward averaging have until 1997 to bring forward averaged amounts back into income.

TAX TIP If you are in the lowest or in the middle tax bracket this year, bring forward averaged amounts back into your income. If you are in the top bracket, investigate ways to lower your income in a particular year so that you can drop into the middle or lowest tax bracket.

Alternative Minimum Tax

Much to the chagrin of tax professionals and a handful of taxpayers, the Alternative Minimum Tax (AMT) was not a casualty of tax reform. The system is complex. Stripped to the bare essentials, you may be subject to the AMT if your total federal tax payable is less than about 17% of your gross income in excess of $40,000. Gross income is income before you deduct amounts for most RRSP and pension plan contributions, tax shelters, real-estate losses and the non-taxable portion of capital gains. Any AMT you pay in excess of your standard tax liability is refundable in any of the next seven years when you are not subject to the AMT.

When figuring out your AMT, you have to perform two separate tax calculations and reconcile the two. There are two rules of thumb for the AMT. One, if you are normally in the top tax bracket and are pleased with the small amount of tax that you owe this year, you may have an AMT problem. Two, anybody who thinks that they may be subject to the AMT should get professional advice. There may be more effective ways to structure your financial affairs so that you can avoid AMT problems.

3
Other Tax Credits and Tax Deductions

Structurally, the new tax credits differ from the old deductions. Instead of writing eligible expenses off against income for tax purposes, you generally claim 17% of the expense as a credit against federal tax owing. Since provincial tax is based on federal tax owing after making the tax credit claim, the credits in effect also reduce your provincial tax bill. Thus, the actual value of the credits is generally about 26%—17% federal tax plus about 9% provincial tax.

As might be expected, not all tax credits are created equal. Some are more beneficial than others. Some disappear when your income reaches a certain level. And several are transferable. All can be used to reduce your tax bill by substantial amounts if you know the rules of the game.

Medical Expense Tax Credit

Medical expenses incurred in a twelve-month period ending in the year are eligible for the tax credit. Expenses for which you are reimbursed, either by your employer or a private or government-sponsored health care plan, are not eligible for the credit. Fees paid to a private health or dental plan, or such fees that appear on your T-4 from your employer as taxable benefits, are eligible for the credit. Fees paid to a Government plan, or paid on your behalf by your employer and included in your income as taxable benefits, are not eligible for the tax credit.

The list of eligible expenses is almost endless. If you have any doubt, check Interpretation Bulletins IT-339R and IT-509, both of which are available from your District Taxation Office. Don't forget that most dental bills also qualify.

The credit is calculated as 17% of your eligible expenses. However, your expenses must first be reduced by the lesser of $1,500 or 3% of net income as reported in your tax return to determine the eligible amount. Thus, if you have $1,900 in eligible expenses and your net income is $37,000, you will be able to claim a medical tax credit of $134.30 against federal tax, determined as follows: $1,900 – 3% of $37,000 = $1,900 – $1,110 = $790 × 17% = $134.30.

TAX TIP It can pay to get your eligible medical expenses out of the way in one fell swoop, or at least over a specific twelve-month period. For example, assume that you have already accumulated $2,000 of expenses over the last ten months, but only $500 is eligible for the credit because of the 3% of net income limitation. Both your children need extensive dental work. If the work is done over the next two months, the expense is added on to the eligible $500 this year so that all of the dental expense is eligible for the credit. If you wait three or four months, up to $1,500 of the dental expense will not be allowed in the following year.

Either spouse may claim a tax credit for the medical expenses of the other, no matter how much income each earns. You or your spouse may also claim the expenses for dependent children or other persons for whom you are entitled to claim a dependant tax credit. Considering the 3% of net income limitation, it will obviously be advantageous for the spouse with the lower net income to claim a credit for medical expenses. This spouse must also claim the dependants' tax credits.

The fact that the higher-income spouse must include family allowance payments in income does not mean that this spouse must claim the dependant tax credits. Remember that now that personal exemptions have been replaced by tax credits, there is no advantage to the spouse in the higher tax bracket claiming tax credits.

Disability Tax Credit

If a child or grandchild of you or your spouse is dependent on you by reason of "mental or physical infirmity", you may be entitled to this tax credit. The credit is also available for dependent parents, grandparents, brothers, sisters, uncles, aunts, nieces and nephews, as long as they reside in Canada at any time in the year.

The definition of mental or physical infirmity has been broadened considerably in the last few years. Generally, the dependant's daily living activities must be "markedly restricted" and the disability must continue or be expected to continue over a twelve-month period. A doctor must certify the disability on form T2201, which must be filed with your return when you make your first claim. This form is available from your district taxation office, as is Interpretation Bulletin IT-509, which provides more detail on the nature of eligible disabilities.

Charitable Donation Tax Credit

The benefits of charitable giving show up just about everywhere you look, including the bottom line on your tax return. All donations made to registered charities (official receipts must be filed with your tax return), up to a limit of 20% of your net income each year, are eligible for a tax credit. Donations that exceed this limit may be carried forward to any of the next five years. Donations made to the Crown (public art galleries or museums and other Government agencies) are not subject to the 20% of net income limitation.

Donations of certified Canadian cultural property made to designated institutions are subject to special rules. Such property must be certified under the regulations of the Cultural Property Export and Import Act and be of cultural or historical importance to Canada. When making such a gift, you are deemed to have disposed of the property at fair market value, which is also the value of your gift for tax purposes. However, any capital gain arising is exempt from tax, although any loss is subject to the regular tax rules. If you cannot claim a tax credit for the full amount of the gift in the year, any unclaimed portion may be carried back one year and forward five years.

Donations made to certain universities in the United States (the list is quite lengthy) are eligible for the tax credit. However, donations made to other U.S. charities are deductible only from income earned in the U.S. The deduction cannot exceed 20% of your U.S. income.

The tax credit is two-tiered. The first $250 that you donate is eligible for a credit at the rate of 17% (federal) and donations in excess of $250 in any one year earn the credit at the rate of 29% (federal top tax bracket). In other words, the more you donate, the larger your credit. Either spouse may claim the donations of the other, no matter whose name is on the official receipt.

TAX TIP If the combined amount of your donations and your spouse's in any year exceeds $250, the tax savings will be larger if one spouse claims all the donations. Otherwise, the tax savings are the same whether you or your spouse makes the claim.

TAX TIP It pays to make those larger donations in the same year. If you donate $500 this year, $250 of the

donation will be eligible for the tax credit at the 29% (federal) rate. On the other hand, if you donate $250 in December and wait until January to donate the other $250, all $500 earns the credit at only the 17% rate.

There is no onus on you to claim your donations in a particular year. Remember that you can carry unclaimed amounts forward five years. Thus, you could delay making a claim so that more of your donation would be eligible for the 29% tax credit. However, this means that your income would be higher than it otherwise would be and therefore you would be paying more tax that year. Prepaying tax in this manner involves a cost and should be balanced against any future tax savings that you hope to achieve.

Most types of capital property donated to charity are eligible for the charitable contribution tax credit. However, a couple of special rules apply. For example, suppose that you want to donate a cottage you inherited a few years ago to the local non-profit boys and girls club. Unless designated in your tax return, you will be deemed to have disposed of the property to the charity at fair market value and will be liable for tax on any resulting capital gain. This gain is eligible for your lifetime capital gains exemption. However, you may designate the transaction to take place at any value between your cost and fair market value. Now you have to figure out the specific value that is best for your tax situation. If you designate the cottage at too low a value, you will reduce your capital gain, but also reduce the size of your charitable tax credit. If you value it too high, you may end up with an unused charitable donation tax credit and a sizeable capital gain. The fly in the ointment is that you must estimate your income over the next five years since you can carry the donation forward. As well, you must estimate future charitable giving, and also try to figure out how much of your capital gains exemption will be available in each of the next five years. A daunting task indeed, but one that will produce substantial tax saving rewards. It's certainly worth a couple of evenings in front of a calculator.

Political Contribution Tax Credit

The federal Government offers a tax credit for contributions made to federal political parties. Official receipts must be filed with your tax return. The credit reduces only your federal tax bill. Most of the provinces also have tax credit systems in place for political contributions to provincial parties.

The federal credit operates on a sliding scale. The first $100 you contribute is eligible for a tax credit at the rate of 75%, maximum $75. The next $450 contributed earns a credit at the rate of 50% and any contributions in excess of $550 earn credits at the rate of 33⅓%. The maximum credit allowed in any year is $500.

TAX TIP It pays to spread your political contributions out over two years. For example, if you contribute $700 in December, you will earn a federal tax credit of $350. If you contribute half, $350, in December and another $350 in January, your tax credits in the two years will total $400, $200 in each year, assuming no further contributions are made in the second year, for a $50 tax saving ($400 minus $350).

TAX TIP If you and your spouse are taxable, consider splitting your political contribution between the two of you. The same $50 saving as above is available if you each contribute $350 rather than one of you contributing $700.

Tuition Fee and Education Tax Credits

Along with the new tuition fee and education tax credits are several radical changes in the tax rules. First, the credits. The tuition credit (federal) is 17% of eligible tuition fees to the extent that such fees exceed $100. Provincial tax is reduced accordingly. The education credit is 17% of $60 for each month of full-time attendance at a qualifying school.

Next, the new wrinkles. The tuition and education credits are only available for post-secondary tuition fees and approved skills-training courses. The institution will be able to tell the student whether fees generate a credit. Tuition paid to elementary or secondary private schools will no longer produce tax savings.

The two tax credits are transferable from the student to a supporting person, generally a parent or spouse. Only the amount that the student is unable to use to bring his or her tax payable down to zero can be transferred. Most importantly, only a maximum of $600 can be transferred. This will not provide much tax relief if a five-figure tuition fee is paid to a U.S. university.

TAX TIP If you paid tuition in 1987 for a course taken in 1988, and the fee was not deducted in your 1987 tax return, you can elect to have that fee deemed to have been paid in 1988; therefore you will receive a larger tuition fee tax credit.

Old Age and Pension Income Tax Credits

The old age credit, available to taxpayers 65 years of age and over, is worth a $550 reduction in your federal taxes. Don't forget to apply for Old Age Security a few months before you turn age 65.

The pension income tax credit is 17% of the first $1,000 of your qualified pension income to a maximum credit of $170 (federal). Qualified pension income includes periodic payments from pension plans, profit sharing plans and RRSPs. Lump-sum payments do not qualify, neither do Canada Pension Plan or Old Age Security payments.

Both credits are transferable to your spouse if you are unable to use all or a portion of them.

TAX TIP If your spouse is not likely to have any qualified pension income, consider contributing to a spousal RRSP that can then be used to generate at least $1,000 of qualified pension income payable to your spouse. If you are already receiving pension income, but your spouse is not, each year you may be able to transfer up to $6,000 of this income on a tax-free basis to a spousal RRSP from 1989 to 1994 inclusive.

Refundable Sales Tax and Refundable Child Tax Credits

These are the only two refundable credits in the system. If the amount of the credits exceeds your tax payable, the excess is paid to you in the form of a "tax refund"—assuming, of course, that you qualify for the credits in the first place.

The refundable child tax credit is available at the rate of $559 per child in 1988 and is payable to the person who receives family allowance cheques for the child. Total credits are reduced at the rate of $5 for every $100 your total family net income exceeds $24,090. For each child aged six and under in 1988, an additional credit of $100 ($200 after 1988) is available, to be reduced by 25% of the child care deduction claimed in the year (see Chapter 7). Your tax return will lead you through these calculations.

TAX TIP Don't forget to apply for the advance payment on your child tax credits if your family net income in the preceding year is less than two thirds of the current year's threshold amount for reducing the child tax credit

(⅔ of $24,090 = $16,060). If you are eligible but don't apply for the advance, you are in effect making a loan to the Government. There is no doubt about who will put this money to better use.

The refundable sales tax credit is payable at the rate of $70 for each adult and $35 for each dependent child eighteen and under. The credit also may be available if you wholly support a parent, at the $35 rate. The total credit is reduced at the rate of $5 for every $100 of total family net income in excess of $16,000 in 1988.

TAX TIP **By making larger RRSP contributions or otherwise reducing your family net income, you can increase the size of your refundable child tax credits. For example, if you have three children and family income of $52,000, your tax credit is only $281.50, if $559 is payable for each child. By making a $3,000 RRSP contribution, family net income is reduced to $49,000 and your refundable child tax credit is increased by $150. And of course, you get the RRSP tax saving as well.**

Foreign Tax Credit

A non-refundable tax credit is available for income or profits taxes paid to a foreign government. Essentially the credit is equal to the lesser of the foreign tax paid and Canadian tax payable on that income. The actual method of determining the credit can be much more complex. As well, you must perform the calculations on a country-by-country basis, using form T2209 for the federal tax credit and form T2036 to determine the size of your credit for provincial tax purposes. Bear in mind that, to the extent that foreign tax on investment and certain other types of income exceeds 15% of the net or underlying foreign income, the excess is a deduction for tax purposes.

You might want to glance at Interpretation Bulletin IT-270R, but if your affairs are at all complex, you should seek professional advice. Working your way through the Canadian tax system is a daunting task. Trying to figure out how you fit into one or two other tax systems as well is no chore for anyone who values their spare time.

4

Home Sweet Home — Your Principal Residence

Just about everyone agrees that buying a home is the best investment the average Canadian will make. Over the long term, houses have steadily increased in value. Any capital gain that you realize on the sale of your home may be tax-free. And unlike "paper" investments, you can actually live in this one.

If your housing situation is pretty much straightforward — one house that you occupy full-time — your gain on a sale will not attract any tax. However, more and more of us own two homes, or even three. We move fairly often and may be renting out at least one of our dwellings some of the time.

It pays to know the rules if you want to preserve the tax-free status of your principal home and to minimize the amount of tax payable when you sell a second home.

Principal Residence

The tax authorities call the home you occupy your "principal residence". This can be a house, condominium, cottage, mobile home or trailer or even a live-aboard boat — just as long as you occupy it for a portion of the year. A principal residence does not have to be located in Canada.

Included in the definition of principal residence is the land on which it is situated. Generally, only the amount of land necessary to the enjoyment of the home is included in the definition — usually no more than one half hectare (about one acre). Where zoning by-laws required a larger parcel of land to be included with your house at the time of purchase, and current zoning by-laws make it impracticable to divide your lot on the sale, more than one half hectare of land can be included in the definition of a principal residence.

TAX TIP It was only in 1987 that the taxman allowed larger parcels of land to be included in the principal residence definition. This ruling was retroactive to 1982. If you are affected, you ought to request that prior years' tax returns be amended to reflect this ruling (see Chapter 16).

The principal residence tax exemption applies to gains on a year-by-year of ownership basis. It is available to a "family unit" on only one home, in any one particular year or part year, for gains arising since the beginning of 1982. Your family unit consists of yourself, your spouse, if any (you must be married; common-law relationships are not eligible) and your unmarried children under the age of eighteen. Whoever claims the exemption must be a resident of Canada for at least part of each year in which the gain arises.

For gains from the beginning of 1972 to the end of 1981 (capital gains were not taxed before 1972), each individual is entitled to the tax exemption for one house in any particular year. Family status is not a factor for entitlement to the exemption.

So what do these complicated-sounding rules mean to an average homeowner? An example or two will help to explain them. Let's assume that you bought your home in 1983 for $65,000 and you sold it in 1988 for $145,000, occupying it continuously during this period. Your capital gain is $80,000 ($145,000 minus $65,000). Capital gains are discussed in Chapter 14.

To determine how much of your gain is exempt you use

the following standard formula: one plus number of years of occupancy *designated by you* (you may not want to designate all of the years you have occupied the dwelling), divided by number of years of ownership. You multiply this fraction by the gain to determine the exempt amount. In this case, the entire gain would be exempt using the following numbers in the formula: (1 + 5)/6 × $80,000 = 1 × $80,000 = $80,000. The "one plus" in the formula allows for the purchase and sale of a home in one year, since that same year will have to be used in the calculation of the gain on both homes.

If you co-own the house with your spouse, you generally must share the gain, but you are each entitled to a principal residence designation in each year on the same house. For years after 1981, if one of you designates the city home for a particular year, the other cannot designate a vacation home for those same years. Remember that the decision to designate a home need only be made when you file your tax return for the year the home is sold.

Let's change the example a bit and assume that you have owned the home since 1976, when you bought it for $32,000. Now you have owned the home for thirteen years inclusive. Your entire gain, $113,000, is still exempt using the following numbers in the formula: (1 + 12)/13 × $113,000 = 1 × $113,000 = $113,000.

Let's make the example a bit more typical and introduce a second home, say a cottage that you use in the summer. This qualifies as a principal residence and any gains on sale may be exempt under the principal residence rules, even if you rent the cottage occasionally (see below). We will assume that you bought the cottage at the same time as the house—in 1976—and you paid $19,000 for it. You sell it in 1988 for $71,000, and therefore your gain is $52,000. To simplify matters we will assume that you have been the sole owner of the city home while your spouse has been the sole owner of the cottage since the date of purchase.

Now you have a choice to make. As explained above, you and your spouse are each entitled to a principal residence designation for gains arising in years before 1982. Therefore the gains on both properties from 1976 to the end of 1981 inclusive (six years) are exempt. However, both of you must designate the same property in any particular year for gains arising after 1981. Obviously, the property with the larger gain after 1981 (the city home) should be designated, which means a portion of the gain arising after 1981 on the cottage may be taxable.

To determine the taxable portion, you can use one of two methods. The standard formula may be used, but you are not allowed to add one year to the number of years designated. Thus, the exempt portion of the total gain of $52,000 on the cottage would be $24,000: 6/13 × $52,000 = $24,000. Therefore, $28,000 of the gain is taxable and must be included in your spouse's income. Determining the exempt portion of the gain using the second method requires that you know the value of the cottage on December 31, 1981. Let's say it was $33,000, which means that a gain of $14,000 arose before 1982. This would be the exempt portion using the second method, leaving $38,000 taxable (gain of $52,000 minus exempt portion of $14,000). Obviously you would choose to use the first method to calculate the exempt portion of the gain. Bear in mind that to even use the second method, you must go to the expense of having an appraisal of the cottage's 1982 value.

In this situation, the $28,000 gain would be eligible for the $100,000 lifetime capital gains exemption, which brings up the tricky question of ownership. For gains arising before 1982, there is a definite advantage to one spouse owning one home and the other spouse owning the other home. Co-ownership at the time of sale can produce a king-size tax headache. Why? Because even though each spouse can designate a home for the principal residence exemption, each can designate only one home in a particular year. If they co-own both homes, half the gain on each home or the entire gain on one home becomes taxable.

Fortunately, the solution to this potential problem is sanctioned by the tax authorities. You are permitted to transfer your share of the ownership in a home to your spouse at any time—but definitely before any sale—and the effective date of the transfer will be considered the date you purchased the home. The transfer must be made at cost, not at fair market value. Your spouse will then be able to designate for all the years you were able to designate, and vice versa. Thus, the gains on both homes to the end of 1981 will be exempt.

While there may not seem to be much incentive for one-person ownership for gains arising after 1981, since each spouse must designate the same home in a particular year, tax savings still could be available if home ownership is structured properly.

TAX TIP If you own two properties, generally the spouse with the lower marginal tax rate should own the property on which the taxable gain will arise, that is, the property with the smaller gain. However, you should also take account of which spouse will benefit the most by claiming all or a portion of the gain on the home under his or her $100,000 lifetime capital gains exemption.

If you own two homes and are selling only one, you will be faced with a different set of concerns. Essentially, you can choose to designate the home being sold as your principal residence, in which case the entire gain would be exempt. Or you can choose to save your designation for the other home when you eventually sell it. On the surface, your decision looks easy. You calculate the actual gain on the house being sold, the accrued gain on the other home, compare the two and either use or save your designation. The decision may not be this easy, however, since by saving your designation you either pay tax on your gain or use your capital gains exemption.

Prepaying tax is costly. In fact, at a 10% interest rate, prepaying $1,000 of tax today is about the same as paying $2,000 of tax in seven years. This is simply another way of saying that if you kept the $1,000 and earned interest at a 10% rate after tax, you would accumulate $2,000 that could be used to pay your tax bill in seven years time.

Using your $100,000 lifetime capital gains exemption when you don't have to could also involve a cost, although you may need a crystal ball to put it in dollars and cents. There may, however, be ways of avoiding difficult decisions like these.

TAX TIP Consider placing ownership of your second home in the names of your children who are eighteen years of age or older, or even in the names of your parents. If they have no principal residence of their own and occupy the second home occasionally, they should be eligible for the exemption for each year of ownership. Beware, however, that you would no longer own the property and therefore may have no control over its sale, or even the eventual transfer to you on the death of your parents.

It is common for a person selling one house and buying another to take back a mortgage on the old home and mortgage the new one for a higher amount than intended. In this situation, the interest from the mortgage taken back must be included in income. Unfortunately, no deduction is allowed for the extra interest that is paid on the new mortgage. It seems unfair, but those are the rules.

That's not to say that there are not a couple of ways you might get around this expensive dilemma. You might consider selling the mortgage on the old home. You will probably lose a few dollars on the transaction, since we suspect the interest rate might be a bit lower than current rates and mortgages are usually sold at a small discount. You should compare the tax cost of holding the mortgage against the costs of selling it.

If you have sufficient funds in your RRSP, you might consider lending these funds to the purchaser in the form of a mortgage. The interest would then be payable to your RRSP, and of course no tax is payable on interest income in an RRSP (see Chapter 5).

Many people buy a plot of land, but do not build on it until a few years later. You should note that any gain accrued on the land up to the time you occupy your home is not eligible for your principal residence exemption. Of course, when eventually realized, this capital gain is eligible for your lifetime $100,000 capital gains exemption. The trick is to find out what the land was worth immediately before you occupied the home so that you can determine the size of your capital gain. Talk to your real-estate agent first.

Don't forget that any expenditure that adds to the lasting value of an asset is added to the cost of that capital asset. For example, assume that you add two bedrooms to your cottage and winterize it. When it comes time to sell the cottage and calculate your capital gain, these expenditures are added to your cost, which in turn reduces your capital gain.

Problems crop up when you try to draw a line between capital expenditures and ordinary expenses. Your expenditures on the cottage were obviously capital in nature—they imparted lasting value to the asset, even though the value of the asset might eventually decline, and they would not be classified as repairs. On the other hand, repairing a leaky roof or painting the kitchen would obviously be classified as ordinary repairs and maintenance. If in doubt, keep your receipts —forever. You never know when you might sell. If you don't sell and your children inherit the property, the increase in cost should help to reduce taxes at the time of your death.

As well, consider keeping the receipts for expenditures on each home that you own. It's possible that it may work to your advantage to claim the principal residence exemption on your vacation property, and realize a capital gain on your city home.

It is not unusual for a husband and wife to have each owned a home before marriage and to continue to own the homes during the marriage. In this situation, one of the most common questions asked is how the principal residence exemption works when it comes time to sell both homes.

For each year or part year that you owned the home when you were not married, you each may claim the exemption. However, you are entitled to designate only one home for each year of your marriage after 1981. Thus, one of your homes will be entirely exempt from tax but it will not be possible to avoid recognizing a gain on the other home. You will get the advantage of the "plus one" in the principal residence formula, which will reduce your capital gain to some extent, and of course, the gain is eligible for your lifetime $100,000 capital gains exemption.

If you happen to split up and go back to each owning a home, once again you each become entitled to the principal residence exemption, but only for years that you lived separate and apart for the entire year, according to a court order or written agreement (see Chapter 14 for information on separation and divorce).

Change in the Use of Your Home

Generally speaking, the principal residence exemption is available for each year or part-year that you occupy your home. If you rent out your home, or rent out an apartment in your home, the principal residence exemption is not available. As with many tax rules, this one is chock full of exceptions and elections that you can make to prevent any unpleasant tax consequences.

Let's start with the most common situation. You take up work in another city, and instead of selling your home, you rent it out. Three years later, you move back to the city and reoccupy your home. Do you lose the principal residence exemption for these three years? No. You may elect in your tax return (a simple letter stating that you are making the election will suffice) to have the home considered your principal residence for those years. You make the election in the year you move out and begin renting the home.

Once the election is made, up to four consecutive years will be exempt under the principal residence rules. It does not matter whether you move to another city, or simply move into an apartment and begin renting your old home. If you are transferred by your employer to another city and you eventually reoccupy the home when still employed by that employer, or in the following year, there is no time limit during which the election will be in force.

To maintain principal residence status in either situation, you may not claim capital cost allowance (depreciation) on the home while it is being rented. This will not prove to be a great hardship since you may claim depreciation at the rate of only 4% a year, and only on the building, not on the land. In many cities, the land under an average older home is worth much more than the building. In addition, you must continue to be a Canadian resident for the period during which you did not occupy the home in order to claim the principal residence designation.

What happens if you bought a home several years ago as a rental property, but later decide to move in? The rules are a bit more complicated in this situation. You are deemed to have disposed of the home in the year you occupy it and must recognize any resulting capital gain for tax purposes. The gain is eligible for your lifetime capital gains exemption. Remember, however, that if tax is payable, the cash must be raised from other sources, since you have not actually sold the property.

Fortunately, relief is available. You can elect to have this "deemed disposition" not occur, and can defer recognizing the gain for tax purposes until you sell the house. You make the election retroactively in the year you occupy the home. As well, if you have made the election, you may use your principal residence designation for up to four years for the period during which the home was a rental property. You may not make the election if you have claimed capital cost allowance on the home in any year after 1984.

For example, suppose that you rented the home for six years after buying it, and then occupied it yourself for four years before selling it. Only one tenth of the gain would be taxable, using the formula: 1 + 4 years of occupancy + 4 years elected divided by 10 years of ownership. Thus, nine tenths of the gain would be exempt under your principal residence exemption.

If you own a duplex, the rules are quite similar. Just think of the rental portion as a separate home. If you rent out part of your home during the entire time you are living there, your principal residence exemption will only apply to the portion of the gain on the home that relates to the part you occupy. The other portion of the gain must be recognized for tax purposes, although it is eligible for your lifetime $100,000 capital gains exemption. The rental portion must be self-contained for this rule to apply. If you are renting out only a room with no cooking facilities, the entire gain on the home will be eligible for your principal residence exemption.

If you convert the rental apartment to living space for yourself, or if you turn part of your home into a self-contained rental unit, rules similar to those above apply for converting an entire home. However, if you make an election when you commence to rent out the unit, you will not be eligible for the extension past four years since you did not move out of the home.

These rules for part of a residence apply whether you are earning rental income or are using part of the home for a business.

Farm Property

Farm houses are also eligible for the principal residence exemption. Since the farm land and often the farm house are used for business purposes (farming), a specific option applies. When you sell the farm, including the farm house, you may choose to calculate your principal residence exemption according to the following formula: $1,000 plus $1,000 times each year of ownership after 1971. Thus, if you sell the farm in 1989 and you owned it since 1965, $19,000 of your capital gain would be exempt ($1,000 plus $1,000 times 18 years—1972 to 1989 inclusive).

You can also use the normal rules and include no more than ½ hectare of land as part of your principal residence. However, if you have used the farm house extensively for the business of farming and have deducted business expenses relating to the house, you may have to pro-rate your principal residence claim, in which case the optional treatment may work to your benefit.

Foreign Residences

Any home that you normally occupy, even on a seasonal basis for only part of the year, qualifies for your principal residence exemption—including homes in another country. Bear in mind that you must be a Canadian resident for years designated under the principal residence rules.

Of course, this exemption will not affect any foreign tax liability that you may incur when you sell your foreign home. In fact, if the foreign tax liability is relatively large, you may be better off not claiming the exemption, nor the capital gains exemption, if you will be entitled to foreign tax credits in your Canadian tax return. Generally this will only be the case if the foreign tax is an income or profits tax. This is the case for federal tax levied in the United States.

If your tax bill is going to be relatively large, you will probably benefit from professional advice in this area. You have enough trouble keeping your tax bill down in one country. Why pay too much tax to two countries?

In particular circumstances, there could be an advantage in having a corporation that you control own your foreign residence.

5
Registered Retirement Savings Plans (RRSPs)

Most of us have contributed to an RRSP for one reason or another. Often we contribute because of the tax saving that we see in the form of a larger refund cheque in the spring. Or some of us use RRSPs to shelter investment income from tax. And many Canadians without access to a company sponsored pension plan use RRSPs to save for their retirement.

These are precisely the reasons why RRSPs have taken the Canadian investment scene by storm over the past decade. Are they as good as everybody seems to think? For most Canadians, there is little doubt that the answer is a resounding yes.

Pre-tax Dollars in Your RRSP Mean Big Savings

What can the average Canadian expect from an RRSP savings program? First, the fact that you can put pre-tax dollars to work for you in the RRSP means larger accumulations. Let's assume that your marginal tax rate is 40% and you contribute \$3,000 to an RRSP. This produces a \$1,200 tax saving, which could also be contributed to the RRSP to produce another tax saving. Instead, let's assume that you make a pre-tax contribution of \$5,000. This in effect produces a \$2,000 tax saving (40% of \$5,000). Thus your contribution consists of the \$2,000 tax saving and \$3,000 of after-tax income. In other words, you have pre-tax income working for you earning investment dollars.

Now let's assume that your RRSP has doubled in value over a seven-year period, which means that it has earned about 10% each year. So today it's worth $10,000. If you were to cancel the RRSP, tax would be payable on the entire amount at your 40% marginal rate. Thus, tax of $4,000 would be payable, leaving you with $6,000. In other words, the after-tax amount that you contributed to the RRSP has also doubled in value, as has your deferred tax liability.

Compare this with investing after-tax dollars outside an RRSP. Your $3,000 will earn 10% interest each year, but tax will be payable on these earnings, cutting your annual interest rate to 6%. It will take about twelve years for your $3,000 to double in value, instead of the seven years it takes with the RRSP. By deferring tax and putting all your pre-tax dollars to work with the RRSP, you end up much further ahead.

And how well off will you be with a long-term RRSP program? As a very rough rule of thumb, if you can contribute 1% of your pre-tax income each year for about 35 years, the RRSP will replace about 10% of your average pre-retirement income, if the RRSP earns income at average long-term interest rates. Thus if you contribute, say, 7% of your pre-tax income each year, the RRSP could fund as much as 70% of your retirement income, the other 30% coming from the Canada Pension Plan and Old Age Security. Bear in mind that the RRSP retirement income would not be indexed to compensate for increases in the inflation rate.

Three important points should be noted. First, the rule of thumb assumes that you contribute each and every year for 35 years. Second, it assumes that you contribute 1% of your pre-tax earnings each year, not a fixed dollar amount. And third, you must leave all the funds in the RRSP for the 35 years. It is the contributions made in the first few years that really make the difference in the size of your retirement income. You can accumulate just as much in an RRSP by your 65th birthday by contributing for eight years from age 25 to 32 as by contributing for 32 years from age 33 to 64.

Contributing to Your RRSP

As you are probably aware, the RRSP rules are slated to change under pension reform. Most of the changes take effect in 1990. But first we will look at the "old" rules that still apply for 1988 and 1989. The "new" rules are summarized later in this chapter.

Anybody who has "earned income" in a particular year is entitled to make an RRSP contribution. However, you may not contribute to your own RRSP past the age of 71, since your RRSP must be converted to a retirement-income vehicle by the end of the year in which you turn age 71. You may, however, contribute to your spouse's RRSP if he or she is younger than you and therefore still eligible to have an RRSP (see below). Earned income includes:

- ☐ Employment income,
- ☐ Income from carrying on a business, either alone or as a partner actively engaged in the business,
- ☐ Rental income from real property,
- ☐ Royalties in respect of a work or invention of which the taxpayer is the author or inventor,
- ☐ Research grants, net of expenses,
- ☐ Alimony and maintenance payments and
- ☐ Most types of retirement or pension payments, including RRSP payments.

Minus

- ☐ Losses from carrying on a business or the rental of real property,
- ☐ Deductible alimony or maintenance payments and
- ☐ Non-taxable transfers between retirement plans.

If you are a member of a Registered Pension Plan (RPP) or a Deferred Profit Sharing Plan (DPSP) and benefits accrued under the plan during the year, you may contribute 20% of your earned income up to a maximum of $3,500, minus your own deductible contributions to the RPP. If you are not a member of an RPP or DPSP, the maximum you may contribute to an RRSP is $7,500.

The "New" Contribution Rules

The maximum that you may contribute to an RRSP beginning in 1990 is 18% of your earned income in the previous year, up to a prescribed maximum amount. Beginning in 1990, earned income will no longer include any type of retirement or pension payment or benefit, including retiring allowances, death benefits and amounts received from an RRSP. Transfers between retirement plans will not generally be included in income and therefore do not figure in the calculation of earned income.

In 1990, the maximum annual contribution is $10,500. This increases to $15,500 in 1995, after which it is indexed according to increases in the average industrial wage. If you are a member of an RPP or a DPSP, the maximum that you may contribute to an RRSP is reduced. Thus, to make the maximum $10,500 contribution in 1990, your earned income in 1989 will have to be at least $58,335, and you could not have been a member of an RPP under which you accrued benefits in the year or a member of a DPSP to which contributions were made.

If you are a member of an RPP or a DPSP at any time in 1990, your RRSP contribution limit will be reduced by a "Pension Adjustment" or PA. The PA is a measure of the benefit that accrues to you under the benefit provisions of an RPP or DPSP in the year. The theory is that if you are the recipient of tax assistance in respect of an RPP or DPSP (remember that your employer deducts any contributions made to a plan on your behalf), the tax assistance you receive in respect of an RRSP should be reduced accordingly.

The principle is fair and makes perfect sense, but putting it into action is another matter. Fortunately almost all the dirty work is left to employers and the Government.

If you are a member of a *money purchase* RPP or a DPSP, your PA is simply the total of all contributions made by you and your employer to these plans. If you belong to a *defined benefit* RPP, your PA reflects the benefits that you accrue under the plan in the year; the amount of actual employer and employee contributions does not enter into this calculation. With a money purchase RPP, specific amounts are contributed each year and the best possible pension is purchased with the accumulated funds when the individual retires. With a defined benefit plan, the more common type, a specific pension is promised to be paid, and the employer and usually the employee make sufficient contributions to fund these pension benefits.

Determining a PA for members of defined benefit RPPs promises to be a daunting task. Fortunately, your employer will report your PA each year on your T-4, enabling you to make your RRSP contribution relatively early in the year with little fear of overcontributing to the RRSP and incurring possible penalties.

The year 1990 also marks the first time that you may carry forward your RRSP contribution limit to a future year. If for some reason you do not contribute the maximum to which you are entitled, you may make up for the shortfall in any of the following seven years. For example, suppose that you can contribute $8,000 in 1990, but you only contribute $5,000. In 1991 you contribute $7,000, but have a $9,000 limit. When you make your 1991 contribution, the first $3,000 that you contribute will relate to 1990, so that you will have entirely used up your 1990 RRSP "room". The other $4,000 relates to 1991, and you will carry forward $5,000 to the next year ($9,000 limit minus $4,000 contribution that relates to 1991).

To complicate matters further, your RRSP contribution limit may be adjusted in a number of circumstances. For example, if you leave a pension plan and either transfer amounts to another plan or receive a refund of your contributions, a Pension Adjustment Reversal (PAR) may result. This would happen if the PAs that you had been charged were greater than the money that you received from the pension plan that you left. Essentially, PARs mean that your RRSP limit may be restored. A Past Service Pension Adjustment (PSPA) may result if your pension plan is retroactively upgraded to provide better benefits, in which case your total RRSP limit will be reduced. A PSPA could result if you transfer benefits to a new plan and purchase additional past service benefits. However, you are only allowed to benefit from an upgrade or from additional benefits to the extent of your available RRSP contribution room plus $8,000 (see Chapter 6).

TAX TIP There is no carry forward of unused RRSP deduction room for 1988 and 1989. You should consider contributing the maximum allowed, even if you have to borrow the funds.

When and What to Contribute

You may make a contribution for a particular year at any time in that year and during the first 60 days of the following year. In 1988 and 1989, this deadline is as crucial as it has always been. You cannot make up for amounts that you neglected to contribute. However, beginning in 1990, unused RRSP deduction room can be carried forward for up to seven years, so the deadline will not mean a great deal, at least until the end of February in 1998 when unused room from 1990 will first expire.

TAX TIP The earlier in the year you contribute to your RRSP, the better off you will eventually be. By contributing in January or February every year, instead of waiting until the end of the year or the following 60 days, you can accumulate up to 10% more in your RRSP, which means your retirement income gets a 10% boost.

You may of course contribute cash to your RRSP, but you may also contribute other "property" as long as it qualifies as an RRSP investment (see below). If you contribute property, such as stock or bonds, you are deemed to have disposed of the property at fair market value immediately before ownership is transferred to your RRSP (your RRSP is like a separate person for tax purposes and can own property). This is the value ascribed to your RRSP contribution. A gain that results on the disposition must be taken into account for tax purposes. Any capital loss is denied.

TAX TIP Do not transfer capital property with accrued losses to your RRSP. You will be better off to sell it at arm's length, in which case you will be able to recognize the loss and apply it against any capital gains.

RRSPs are not strictly retirement plans. You may withdraw funds from your plan at any time, if you are willing to suffer the tax consequences. (Employee or group RRSPs may be subject to a locking-in feature that restricts your access to the plan funds.) Any amount withdrawn in a year must be included in your income for tax purposes. Tax will be withheld by the issuer of the RRSP, so you will not receive the full amount, but credit for this tax is given when you file your return.

TAX TIP If you need the funds in your RRSP, for example, to fund the downpayment on your first home, try to arrange the withdrawal in a year when your income is unusually low. You may be able to avoid some or all of the tax that would normally be payable. However, it probably won't pay in the long run to withdraw RRSP funds just because you are not taxable in a particular year. You cannot put those funds back into the RRSP, so you permanently lose the tax shelter aspects of the RRSP.

TAX TIP If you plan to take up residence in another country, you may be better off leaving your RRSP intact, and then cancelling it once you are no longer a resident of Canada. You will generally have to pay a non-resident withholding tax of 25% on the entire amount but this may be the least expensive way to gain access to your RRSP funds. As well, tax treaties may reduce the 25% withholding rate, and in some cases you may be able to eliminate Canadian tax altogether. Professional advice is a must in this situation.

If you borrow to make an RRSP contribution, the interest expense on the loan is not deductible for tax purposes.

TAX TIP If you borrowed for an RRSP contribution that was made before November 12, 1981, and the loan is still outstanding, the interest may still be deductible. Non-deductible debt should be paid off before this one. Then pay off other debt on which the interest is deductible, so that your ability to control the cost of borrowing is maintained.

After 1989, a penalty will apply at any point in time you exceed your total RRSP contribution limit by more than $8,000. The penalty is 1% per month of your "cumulative excess amount" at the end of the month. The $8,000 allowance does not apply if the taxpayer is under the age of nineteen. In 1988 and 1989, the penalty applies if you contribute more than your annual limit if your limit exceeds $5,500; otherwise the limit is $5,500.

TAX TIP You might consider overcontributing to your RRSP by the $8,000 limit, if you were going to invest this sum outside an RRSP in any case. Investment income earned on the $8,000 will not be taxed, and you have the option of deducting the overcontribution at any time as long as you have RRSP contribution room available. For example, you may contribute the maximum of $10,500 to your RRSP in 1990 and overcontribute by another $8,000. In 1991, your RRSP deduction limit is $11,500, but you only have enough cash to contribute $3,500. Nevertheless, you can claim a deduction for the entire $11,500, which includes the $8,000 contributed in 1990.

Note that there is a possibility that intentional overcontributions to an RRSP could be attacked under the new General Anti-Avoidance Rules (GAAR).

Spousal RRSPs

You may contribute to your spouse's RRSP within your own limits. The two of you must actually be married—a common-law spouse does not count as a "spouse" in this particular situation.

TAX TIP You should definitely plan to make spousal RRSP contributions if there is any chance that your retirement income will be considerably larger than your spouse's. By shifting your income into your spouse's hands, you should be able to eventually lower your family tax bill during your retirement years—perhaps by a substantial amount.

A special rule prevents abuse of the spousal contribution privilege. If your spouse withdraws funds from a plan to which you have contributed in the current year or immediately preceding two years, other than by way of a retirement income, the amount withdrawn will be included in your income and not in your spouse's income. Thus, your spouse should consider making his or her own contributions to one RRSP, while you make spousal contributions to a separate plan, just in case it becomes necessary to tap an RRSP for funds. The person with the lower marginal tax rate would make the withdrawal, assuming both of you had RRSPs.

Since most provinces require at a minimum the division of family assets on the breakdown of a marriage, and RRSPs are generally considered to be a family asset, you shouldn't hesitate to contribute to a spousal RRSP. Chances are good, at least statistically, that your marriage will survive and that you will be better off during your retirement years because of having made the spousal RRSP contributions. If your marriage fails, these RRSP assets were probably going into the communal pot in any case. Chapter 14 discusses the tax consequences of splitting up RRSP assets on separation or divorce.

Special Transfers to RRSPs

Pension reform will curb the flexibility of RRSPs to some extent. In the past it has been possible to transfer a variety of "pension" amounts to an RRSP on a tax-free basis. This allowed taxpayers to continue to shelter pension income from tax. Beginning in 1990, only lump-sum direct transfers from RPPs and DPSPs will be allowed. The tax-free transfer of retiring allowances will continue to be allowed, but only up to $2,000 for each year of service, plus $1,500 for each year of service before 1989 that the individual was not a member of an RPP or DPSP.

TAX TIP **Since 1989 is the last year you will be able to defer regular payments received from pension plans, DPSPs, RRSPs, the Canada/Quebec Pension Plans and Old Age Security in sizeable amounts, consider transferring as much as possible to your RRSP. In this way, you will be able to augment your retirement income in later years. It may be worthwhile selling some of your investments now to make up for any cash shortfall in the year.**

TAX TIP **Consider transferring up to $6,000 of your pension income to a spousal RRSP each year beginning in 1989, if you do not otherwise need the funds. Only periodic payments received from an RPP or DPSP qualify. This provision will be available only until 1994. After that date, it will be impossible to defer pension income even though you may have no immediate need for the funds.**

While these special transfers are deductible for regular income tax purposes, they are not deductible when you are calculating your alternative minimum tax liability. If you do become subject to the AMT, you will, in effect, be paying tax on the amounts transferred, although in a following year, you will likely be refunded this tax. It will generally pay to make the transfer, even though you may wind up with an AMT problem. You might want to have a professional review your options and determine the potential tax savings, or perhaps tax cost.

RRSP Investing

An RRSP can be either an investment or an investing vehicle. For example, you can buy a Guaranteed Income Certificate (GIC) wherever you bank and choose to have it registered as an RRSP. You can also open up a self-directed RRSP (see below), contribute the appropriate amount of cash to the plan and arrange for the RRSP to purchase the GIC. RRSPs purchased from an insurance company can be considered a third type. They have several unique features, although for the most part they are similar to the basic type of RRSP.

Most financial institutions sell or issue RRSPs, and they will also set up self-directed plans.

The list of investments that qualify as RRSP investments is lengthy. It includes money, most debt instruments, including GICs, bonds, term deposits and stripped bond coupons, shares, most warrants and certain types of options, mortgages and even the mortgage on your own home. Precious metals, such as gold or silver, and shares in corporations with which you do not deal at arm's length do not qualify as RRSP investments. As well, no more than 10% of the cost of your RRSP investments in a self-directed plan may be invested in foreign qualifying securities, although this limit may be increased if you invest in eligible small businesses. The penalty for holding non-qualified investments in your RRSP can be severe.

Unless you have a self-directed RRSP, you will be limited in your choice of RRSP investments to the common debt securities – savings accounts, term deposits, GICs and mutual funds. If purchased from a bank or most trust companies, these investments are covered by the $60,000 Canada Deposit Insurance Program, should the financial institution fail. This $60,000 is in addition to the Canada Deposit Insurance protection you have on your investments outside of an RRSP. Credit unions, caisse populaires in Quebec and insurance companies have their own form of insurance to protect RRSP deposits.

TAX TIP If you have $60,000 on deposit with one financial institution, use another, not just another

branch of the same one, to make further RRSP contributions. The $60,000 limit for Canada Deposit Insurance coverage applies to all branches of the institution and to all deposits made there, not just to individual branches or securities you may have on deposit.

Units or shares in a mutual fund (also called investment funds) may also qualify as RRSP investments, or your self-directed plan can purchase mutual funds. The investments made by the fund itself must be eligible for RRSP purposes.

TAX TIP If you have purchased two or three different mutual funds as RRSP investments, it may pay to open a self-directed plan and transfer the funds into the plan. The annual administration fee you pay to the self-directed plan administrator may be less than the several administration fees you are paying to the different plans, which are not payable if the fund is held by a self-directed RRSP.

Self-directed RRSPs

With a self-directed RRSP, you make the investment decisions, but the administrator, which could be a broker, bank or trust company, carries out your orders and is responsible for safeguarding your RRSP securities. The administrator charges an annual fee, usually in the $100 range. You generally receive monthly reports detailing your investments and transactions.

TAX TIP If you can arrange to pay the administrative fee directly rather than having it deducted from your RRSP balance, the amount is deductible for tax purposes. Many mutual funds that are RRSP investments give you this same option.

One of the main reasons for opening a self-directed RRSP is the flexibility it gives you. You can diversify your investments, fine tune your risk and carry out your portfolio decisions just as easily as if you were investing outside an RRSP. As well, you must have a self-directed plan to take advantage of being able to invest up to 10% of the cost of your investments in foreign securities. And, you must have a self-directed plan to invest in a variety of RRSP-eligible securities, including stripped bond coupons, Canada Savings Bonds and, of course, publicly traded shares in specific corporations. You will also need a self-directed plan if you want to hold the mortgage on your own home in your RRSP.

TAX TIP **If you plan to borrow money, you might want to consider borrowing from your RRSP in the form of a mortgage on your home. The funds advanced to you by your self-directed RRSP are secured by a mortgage on your home. The interest and principal are paid to your RRSP. The terms of the mortgage and the interest rate must be similar to mortgages commercially available at the time. If you use the proceeds of the loan to purchase investments or provide financing for a business, the interest paid on the mortgage to your RRSP should be deductible for tax purposes. For this technique to work successfully, generally you should have in excess of $50,000 in your RRSP available as mortgage funds.**

TAX TIP **If you are self-employed or own a business, you might consider contributing to an RRSP offered by an insurance company. One of the special features of this type of RRSP is that they are constructed like life insurance and contain annuity-like guarantees. For this reason, they cannot be attacked by creditors should you**

declare bankruptcy. Ordinary RRSPs, on the other hand, can be distributed to a bankrupt's creditors.

RRSP Retirement Income Options

You must arrange to receive a retirement income from the accumulated funds in your RRSP by December 31 of the year you turn age 71. If you do not, your RRSP will be deregistered in the following year, which means the entire amount will be included in income and be taxed at your normal rates.

By arranging to receive a retirement income, the RRSP tax shelter is for the most part retained – only the amounts actually received each year are included in income. Two general options are available.

First, you can arrange to receive either a life or fixed-term annuity. The fixed-term annuity extends to age 90 and may be based on your age or your spouse's age if younger than you. Both types of annuities may be indexed in a variety of fashions so that payments increase each year. Life annuities may be guaranteed for specific periods and joint annuities based on the lives of both you and your spouse may be arranged. It is possible to buy an annuity that may be commuted at your option.

Second, you can choose to establish a Registered Retirement Income Fund (RRIF) with your RRSP funds. A RRIF operates very much like an RRSP, except that instead of contributing to the plan, it pays out amounts to you. Everything must be paid out of the RRIF by the year you turn age 90, or if you so choose, when your spouse turns 90 if he or she is younger than you. A specific minimum amount must be paid each year, but you may withdraw as much as you want at any time. You may have a self-directed RRIF, a mutual fund RRIF, or an RRIF that guarantees to pay a specific interest rate over the life of the plan.

You may have as many annuities and RRIFs as you like. You may even transfer commuted annuity amounts into your RRIF, or arrange to buy an annuity with the funds left in your RRIF at any time.

There is a third RRSP retirement income option—you can simply cancel your RRSPs at any time and suffer the tax consequences. This is generally not recommended, unless the funds can be withdrawn with little or no tax liability (you can do exactly the same thing with a RRIF and end up with much more flexibility). If you are taking up residence in another country, tax may be minimized by withdrawing the funds when you are no longer a Canadian resident. In this latter situation, professional advice should definitely be considered—before you leave Canada on a permanent basis.

RRSP income received from a RRIF or in the form of an annuity or from an insurance company annuity is eligible for the pension income tax credit ($170 federally in 1988). By contributing to a spousal RRSP you will ensure that both you and your spouse gain access to this tax credit.

TAX TIP If you need extra cash in the first few years of retirement, perhaps for an extended vacation, consider converting at least a portion of your RRSP to a RRIF. You can withdraw exactly the amount that you need and leave the rest to earn tax-sheltered income inside the RRIF.

Bear in mind that if you have been contributing to a spousal RRSP, any RRIF payments made to your spouse from this plan in excess of the minimum amount required to be paid each year will be included in your income and be subject to tax, to the extent of your spousal RRSP contributions made in the current year and previous two years. Thus, if your marginal tax rate is higher than your spouse's, you will be paying excess tax. Don't forget why you made the spousal RRSP contributions in the first place. Look for other sources to finance the vacation. It may even be worthwhile borrowing if absolutely necessary, rather than raiding your spouse's RRIF.

6
Employee Deferred Income Plans

Most Canadian workers are covered by some type of "pension plan". The emphasis here is on the word "type". Pension plans come in several different types, and there are literally thousands of variations on these. As well, employers sponsor deferred profit-sharing plans, group RRSPs and a variety of employee-benefit plans. Some employees rely on generous retiring allowances to see them through their retirement years, and others may participate in some kind of deferred-compensation or supplementary-pension plan. These plans are now called Salary Deferral Arrangements (SDAs) or Retirement Compensation Arrangements (RCAs) by the Government.

The benefits that you accumulate over the years in a "pension plan" could prove to be among your largest assets—after all, many count on them to provide most of their retirement income, and these days many of us are looking at 20 or 30 years of retirement. Making sure that you are getting the most out of your plan year after year should be at the top of your list of financial priorities.

Registered Pension Plans

There are essentially two types of Registered Pension Plans (RPPs). About 90% of workers covered by a pension plan belong to a defined-benefit RPP of some variety. This type of plan spells out a specific pension benefit that is to be paid on retirement, based on salary and years of service. Generally, you make regular contributions to the plan, while your employer is responsible for making sufficient contributions to ensure that the plan has adequate funding to pay these benefits.

With a money-purchase or defined-contribution RPP, you and your employer contribute specific amounts each year, usually based on wages, and perhaps years of service. The best pension possible is then purchased with the amounts accumulated in the plan.

With a defined-benefit plan, you know in advance approximately what your benefits will be when you retire. They are spelled out in the plan. With a money-purchase plan, you find out what your pension benefits will be at the time you retire. The more that you and your employer contribute to the plan and the better the earnings in the plan, the more will accumulate and the larger will be your retirement income.

Pension Standards and Tax Assistance

Over the past few years, the Canadian pension system has been undergoing a massive overhaul under the banner of pension reform. The process is by no means complete, but many changes have been made. Virtually every worker who is or will become a member of a pension plan is affected in one way or another by the changes made to date. We will only note a few changes that may affect your tax planning this year and next. Your employer should be providing more detail on the many changes your pension plan is likely to undergo.

The pension reform overhaul can be broken down into two broad areas—changes to pension standards and changes to the tax assistance provided by the federal and provincial Governments to encourage retirement saving.

The provinces regulate pension standards, except for federally regulated industries. The new pension standards are in effect in several provinces and federally. Unfortunately, the rules are not perfectly uniform. We only highlight two changes to the standards. First, pension benefits will become much more portable. That is, you will be able to take your accumulated benefits with you when you take a job with a new employer. And since your benefits must now vest within two years, more will be available to take with you to a new plan. Vesting simply means that the benefits arising from your and your employer's contributions belong irrevocably to you.

Second, defined-benefit plans now must offer a greater variety of pension benefits and they must include surviving spouse benefits. It is expected that indexing or inflation protection of pensions will become mandatory in the near future. Choosing one of the new retirement options will generally not be an easy task. You will want to take into account your other sources of retirement income when making the choice. Your major concerns will have to do with your income and expenditures levels ten or twenty years down the road. Predicting these with any degree of accuracy won't be easy, so it may be helpful to get professional advice.

Contributing to Your RPP

The new rules for contributing to pension plans, scheduled for implementation in 1990, are some of the most complex yet written. Fortunately, the onus is generally on employers to deal with the complexities and report the bottom line to employees.

First, since 1986, there have been no limits on how much you may contribute to a defined-benefit RPP and deduct for tax purposes, as long as the contributions are in respect of current service and are required under the plan. Chances are that you are contributing a percentage of salary. That amount is deductible, as long as it is required under the terms of the plan. However, a cap is imposed on how much you and your employer can contribute, since the maximum pension that can be paid from a defined-benefit RPP is limited. This rule will not change in 1990.

Second, and beginning in 1990, the benefits that accrue on your behalf during the year as a result of your participation in your employer's registered plans (RPPs and DPSPs) determine how much you can contribute to RRSPs or to registered plans of another employer. The value of these accrued benefits will be measured by your employer by a PA (Pension Adjustment). For most people, the PA will only directly affect the amounts that may be contributed to RRSPs. The higher your PA, the less you may contribute to an RRSP. This makes sense, since a higher PA means that you are obviously accruing larger benefits in your RPP.

Third, your PA depends on a variety of factors. These were mentioned briefly in the previous chapter on RRSPs.

Your PA essentially measures how your accrued benefits in the year stack up against the maximum allowed. This maximum is based on the maximum annual pension allowed in the first year of retirement, which is the lesser of:

- ☐ 2% times the number of years of pensionable service times the average of the best three consecutive years of salary, and
- ☐ $1,722.22 times the number of years of pensionable service.

If your plan provides three quarters of the maximum benefit, your PA will be roughly three quarters of the maximum (there is a minor adjustment, which is noted below).

We will ignore the complexities of determining the actual dollar figure for your PA—your employer will do that and report to you. Instead, let's go back to the 1990 RRSP contribution limit outlined in the previous chapter, which is 18% of the previous year's earned income minus your PAs for the previous year (you could have more than one if you have more than one employer during the year) plus $600. The $600 is the minor adjustment. It is given to everyone and is designed to compensate for plans that are not as "rich" as others. Your PA uses this same 18% figure as a basis. Assuming your annual salary is $40,000 and you belong to the defined-benefit RPP outlined above that provides three quarters of the maximum benefit, your PA will be three quarters of 18% of $40,000, or $5,400. Thus, a total of $2,400 (18% of $40,000 minus $5,400 plus $600) may be contributed in total to a money-purchase RPP, a DPSP and to your RRSP.

Most employees will belong to one pension plan with one employer during the year. But many belong to combination plans and therefore will have a PA that combines the benefits under all plans of a given employer. Others may belong to an RPP and a DPSP, and still others will change employers and belong to two separate RPPs during the year. Your employer(s) is responsible for reporting your PAs to you along with your T-4 information at the end of February each year. This PA is a global amount that measures your participation in all registered plans of that employer (RPPs and DPSPs). As well, the Government will let you know later in the year how much in total you can contribute to an RRSP.

Money Purchase RPP Contributions

Before 1990, you were limited to contributing a maximum of $3,500 a year to a money-purchase RPP. Those limits are increasing under tax reform. In 1990, if you belong only to a money-purchase RPP, the limit is 18% of your income to a maximum of $11,500, minus the employer's contribution to the money-purchase plan (which in some jurisdictions may have to be at least half the total contribution). The maximum dollar limit increases to $15,500 in 1994 and is indexed thereafter according to increases in the average industrial wage.

If you belong to an RPP that has a defined-benefit promise, as well as a money-purchase component, the benefits accrued under both in any year must not exceed a ceiling measured by the PA. For example, assume that in 1989 you belong to an RPP that provides a 1% defined-benefit promise and also requires you to contribute 4% of your earnings toward a money-purchase component. Your employer is responsible for funding the defined-benefit promise and also for matching your contribution to the money-purchase component. If you earn $40,000 in 1989, your PA under this arrangement will be $3,600 (defined-benefit component) plus $3,200 (money-purchase component) minus $600 = $6,200. You will thus be able to contribute $1,000 to your RRSP for the 1990 taxation year (18% of $40,000 = $7,200 minus $6,200 = $1,000). Your 1990 RRSP contribution limit is determined by your earnings and PA for 1989.

Other Types of Contributions to RPPs

Additional Voluntary Contributions (AVCs) are contributions made under a money-purchase RPP that are not required as a general condition of membership under the plan. A past-service AVC is a contribution made in a given year that relates to service under the plan in a prior year. Current-service AVCs are allowed for 1988 and 1989, but they must be included in your $3,500 limit.

Past-service AVCs made after October 8, 1986, and before 1990 are not deductible. However, if you made a past-service AVC before October 9, 1986, that was not deducted from your income, you have until the end of 1989 to remove the amount from your pension plan with no tax consequences. The undeducted portion of a past-service AVC made before

October 9, 1986, cannot be deducted except in one circumstance. If the undeducted portion of the AVC has been annuitized as retirement income and thus cannot be paid out of the plan, a deduction of up to $3,500 a year is provided against your retirement income.

The new regime continues the prohibition against the deductibility of past-service AVCs that relate to years of service before 1990. Current-service AVCs will be permitted as long as the PA limits are not exceeded.

Past-service AVCs that relate to years of service after 1989 are treated no differently from any other type of past-service upgrade or contribution. These AVCs will result in a PA and thus fit into the new system. The treatment of past-service upgrades and the granting of new past-service are discussed below.

For contributions other than AVCs made after March 27, 1988, in respect of service before 1989, you will be eligible for a deduction of up to $3,500 a year, provided you were not a contributor to any RPP in the particular year of past service. If you contribute more than $3,500, the unused contribution is carried forward to following years when it may be deducted.

For years of service after 1989, any contributions made to the plan for years of past service when you were not a member or certain upgrades to the plan that increase your past-service benefits will effectively result in the PAs of prior years being increased, which means that your RRSP deduction room (see Chapter 5) must be correspondingly reduced to ensure that you do not become entitled to excess tax benefits. The mechanism that reduces your RRSP deduction room is called the Past Service Pension Adjustment (PSPA). Once again, the onus for understanding the mechanism and working with it is on your employer, who will inform you of any changes to your PA or contribution level to the plan or change in your total RRSP deduction room.

You should note that if your plan is upgraded by an indexing or inflation protection feature, a PSPA will not be triggered, and therefore your RRSP deduction room will not be affected. If your plan is already fairly generous, this is probably the most significant past-service benefit upgrade available.

Transfers Between Plans

Under portability provisions of pension reform, RPPs will be required to permit the transfer of accrued benefits to another RPP or to an RRSP. Plans are not, however, required to accept the transfer of benefits from another plan. The transfer must be made directly between plans for it to be tax-free – you cannot get your hands on the money if you want to avoid paying tax on the amount.

The amount of benefits available for transfer depends on whether your pension benefits have vested. Under the new pension-reform standards, benefits must vest within two years of the day you join the plan. If your benefits have not vested, and you leave your employer, you are entitled to receive all your contributions plus a reasonable rate of interest. You will not gain access to any unvested contributions made by your employer. Generally, this amount may be transferred directly to another RPP, if the new plan so allows, or to an RRSP. There may be limitations on the amount that may be transferred to the other RPP or the RRSP, depending on the type of plan that you are leaving and the type of RPP that you are joining. Your employer and the Government will let you know how the rules are to be applied in your particular case.

If your benefits in a defined-benefit plan are already vested, the situation is much more complex. Under the new standards, you will generally have the option of transferring your accrued benefits to a new plan, if that new plan permits such a transfer. You may be able to transfer the full dollar amount of the benefits to an RRSP or leave them in the old plan and collect a pension when you retire. There may, however, be limitations on the amounts that can be transferred. If you are within ten years of the normal retirement date stated in the old plan, you may be able to start receiving a pension that is reduced proportionally to the number of years you are away from the normal retirement date.

To effect a transfer, the present value of your accrued benefits is determined—a complex process (what isn't, with pension plans now?)—and that amount is transferred directly to your new plan. The transfer to an RRSP or money-purchase plan is usually straightforward – the dollar amount is switched over, subject to any applicable limitation. However, if the amount is transferred to a new defined-benefit plan, the new plan must determine what benefits are available for the amount transferred. For example, if you transfer an amount equal to seven years of benefits to a new plan, but the new plan is more generous and the amount results in only six years of benefits being credited to you, you may have the option of buying the seventh year of benefits. If you do, a PSPA will result (see above) and your RRSP deduction room will decrease. If the amount transferred will buy eight years of benefits under the new less generous plan, you may be entitled to a refund, which can be transferred to an RRSP.

If you're confused, don't despair. You're not alone. In fact, it's likely that the growth industry of the 1990s will be the pension-consulting field. In any case, all the work will be done for you, although you must make some far-reaching decisions. For example, you will have to decide if you can do better with an RRSP than with transferring benefits to a new plan, if this option even exists. Comparing the potential benefits is not an easy task. If the amounts are significant, you should consider obtaining professional advice. The size of your retirement income and your comfort for 20 or even 30 years after retiring are at stake.

To show you the kind of issues you will have to consider, let's look at a fairly straightforward hypothetical example. You are warned that the numbers do not reflect any specific situation; they are used simply to demonstrate the kind of complexities with which you could be faced. First, we will assume that for the past eight years, you have belonged to a defined-benefit plan that pays a maximum pension. Assuming that pension reform has been in effect for at least eight years, you have therefore been able to contribute only $600 a year to your RRSP. However, if you had not been a member of the pension plan, you could have contributed another $60,000 to your RRSP over those eight years.

You change jobs and have the option of transferring your benefits to the new RPP, transferring a cash settlement to your RRSP, or leaving your benefits to accrue in the old plan until you retire. If you leave your benefits in the old plan, your pension benefits will be based on the average of your three best consecutive years, which would usually be the three most recent ones. If you choose to transfer your benefits to the new plan, which is identical to the old plan, eight years of benefits will also be based on your best three years, but these will be the three years just before retirement age when you will be making much more than you earn now. Obviously, more cash is needed to fund the benefit in the new plan than the benefit in the old plan. Thus, if you transfer benefits, you will be able to buy, say, only five years of benefits with the cash transferred from the old plan. In other words, you will lose retirement benefits equal to three years of service.

Now let's assume that you opt to transfer the cash value of your benefits to an RRSP. The cash value is $40,000. Since the cash received is less than the PA that you've been charged over the eight years, up to $20,000 of RRSP contribution room is opened up. However, you now have to find the cash to make this catch-up contribution. And if you do, you will still have only $60,000 in your RRSP. If you had been making maximum contributions to your RRSP for the eight years and had not been a member of the RPP, you might have $100,000 in your RRSP by now and perhaps even more.

The conclusion that apparently can be drawn from this example is that it pays to stay with one employer for life, or if you switch jobs often, try not to join a pension plan and instead contribute to RRSPs, assuming that you can negotiate a reasonable salary adjustment. Bear in mind that another example using different pension plans may lead to completely different conclusions. Don't forget that the numbers are used strictly for purposes of the example.

You will have to examine your own situation carefully to determine an appropriate course of action.

Deferred Profit Sharing Plans (DPSPs)

Employees will not be permitted to contribute to a DPSP after 1989. Contributions made before 1990 are not deductible. Employers may contribute up to 18% of the employee's income to a maximum of $5,750 in 1990 (half the limit for total contributions to a money purchase RPP). This maximum will increase to $7,750 by 1994, and be indexed beginning in 1995.

The amount contributed to the DPSP by an employer will

be added to the employee's total PA to determine how much that employee may contribute to an RRSP.

Amounts contributed to a DPSP must vest immediately upon allocation to the employee, if he or she has had two years of service with the employer. Transfers to an RPP, if that RPP so permits, or to an RRSP are allowed, subject to any applicable limitations.

Group RRSPs

These have not been common, but are expected to grow in popularity, primarily because employer costs of supporting and administering a defined-benefit RPP and even a money-purchase RPP are going to increase substantially over the next few years.

On the other hand, a group RRSP is the model of simplicity. The employer contributes a specific amount in respect of the employee to the plan, adds the amount to the employee's income and the employee takes the deduction on his or her tax return. The group RRSP is constructed so that the employee cannot get access to the employer's contributions, called a locked-in RRSP. When the time to retire comes, the amounts accumulated in the name of the employee may be transferred to that employee's own RRSP if he or she so opts, or an RRSP retirement income will be arranged with the amounts.

Generally you will have the option of directly transferring these amounts to a defined-benefit or money-purchase RPP.

Retiring Allowances

Many employees with inadequate pension plans or with years of service when no pension plan was available receive retiring allowances on retirement. These are fully taxable to the employee. However, you can opt to transfer some or all of your retiring allowance to an RRSP within specific limits. The amount transferred will not be subject to tax and will be treated like any other amounts in your RRSP once you make the transfer. Unlike other transfers, this one does not have to be made directly. You have until 60 days after the end of the year in which you receive the retiring allowance to make the tax-free transfer to your RRSP.

For years before 1989, you are permitted to transfer up to $2,000 for each year of service you earned benefits under an RPP or DPSP, plus an additional $1,500 for each year you were not a member of a DPSP or RPP. For years after 1988, the limit is $2,000 per year.

Salary Deferral and Retirement Compensation Arrangements (SDAs and RCAs)

A variety of plans had been developed over the years so that higher-income employees could defer a portion of their wages to later years. Of course tax would also be deferred. Ideally, under these plans, the employer would get an immediate deduction for the amount deferred, although this was not a concern to non-taxable employers such as government agencies or schools.

In 1986, many new rules were introduced to combat virtually any type of salary and tax deferral arrangement not specifically sanctioned under the law. Both unfunded and funded deferred-compensation arrangements may be subject to the general rule for SDAs. In the year the employee has a "right" to the amount in question, a taxable benefit is included in the employee's income. Only when the employee includes the taxable benefit in income does the employer get to deduct the amount. The amount itself is not taxable when eventually received by the employee, since tax would have already been paid on it.

That's the general rule, but of course there are a number of exceptions. If the arrangement contains bona-fide contingencies that clearly establish that the employee has no vested right in the year to receive a payment in the future, the arrangement is not an SDA in that year. Registered plans such as RPPs and DPSPs are not caught by the rules. Neither are certain benefit plans, plans to provide funds for the education of workers and leave of absence plans that are self-funded.

As well, accrued but unpaid bonuses may not be caught by the SDA rules. However, for the employer to deduct the amount, it must actually be paid to the employee within 180 days of the employer's fiscal year end. A one-year deferral is available if the employee actually receives the bonus in the calendar year following the year in which the bonus was earned, although tax must be withheld by the employer on the bonus. Note that the SDA rules will apply if the employee has no right to receive the bonus within three years of the year end.

Some deferral arrangements seek to provide additional benefits upon retirement of an employee. These will generally not fall under the SDA rules, but if they are currently funded, they will be considered an RCA. With an RCA, the employer deducts the amount contributed from income and the employee is not required to include the amount in income for tax purposes. However, for the employer to get the deduction, a special 50% refundable tax must be withheld from the amount and remitted to Revenue Canada when the amount is actually set aside. Earnings on the amount are also subject to a 50% refundable tax. The tax becomes refundable when the amounts are paid to employees. The employee includes the total amount received from the RCA plan (contribution plus earnings) in income.

RCAs will only be viable in isolated circumstances, since

the top combined federal and provincial tax rate is now three or four percentage points lower than 50% in most provinces.

TAX TIP **An employee expecting to give up Canadian residence in the near future should consider an RCA. If the funds are withdrawn after the employee leaves Canada, tax would be levied at 25%. The 50% tax would be completely refunded.**

7
Employee Expenses and Benefits

It's true that employees don't fare as well as the self-employed when it comes to tax-saving deductions and tax-planning possibilities. After all, your employer pays most of your expenses of employment—a place to work, equipment, supplies and a hundred other necessities—and therefore your employer takes the deductions.

Depending on your employer, the nature of your job and your personal situation, a variety of opportunities are waiting for you to exploit. Working parents may be entitled to the child-care expense deduction, which is much more generous this year than previously. If you relocate, you can claim moving expenses. A variety of employee perks may be available that can produce major tax savings.

As you scale the corporate ladder, more and more opportunities will probably appear, especially as you negotiate your remuneration package at the time of promotions, or when you change employers. Two of the most worthwhile opportunities are low-interest or interest-free employee loans and stock-option programs.

Then there is the company car—the most valuable benefit many employees have access to, but also the bane of our tax legislators. The rules for cars have changed almost every year for more than a decade – lately they have been changing almost monthly. Company cars are covered separately in the next chapter.

Child-Care Expenses

Working parents are permitted to deduct the cost of child care from their income for tax purposes within specific limits. The dollar limits were broadened in 1988 in recognition of the increase in child-care costs.

To make a claim for children, they must be under the age of fourteen at some point during the year, or, if older, be dependent because of a mental or physical infirmity. Eligible costs include day care or babysitting, boarding school and camp expenses. Medical expenses, and tuition, clothing or transportation expenses are not eligible for this deduction.

In most cases, the deduction must be claimed by the lower-income spouse. The claim for each child is limited to the lesser of:

- ☐ The amount actually paid,
- ☐ Two thirds of your earned income (which would not include investment income) and
- ☐ $2,000 per eligible child, or $4,000 for each child who is under age seven at the end of the year or who has a severe and prolonged mental or physical impairment.

Beginning in 1988, the $8,000 ceiling on claims has been lifted.

The higher-income spouse may claim the deduction if the lower-income spouse is in school full-time, or for at least two weeks in the year, is either imprisoned or is mentally or physically infirmed. As well, if the couple is separated and living apart at the end of the year and has been for at least three months commencing in the year, the higher-income spouse may claim the deduction. In this case, the above limits apply, and, as well, the deduction may not exceed $60 a week, or $120 a week for children under age seven at the end of the year or who are severely handicapped.

You may not deduct child-care expenses if they are paid to your spouse, a person under 21 related to you or to your spouse, the child's parent, a person who supports the child or a person claimed as a dependant by you. To make your claim, you must report the name, address and social insurance number of persons to whom you make payments.

TAX TIP For child-care payments to be deductible in respect of the current year, they must be made by December 31. If you make January's payment in December, however, you are not permitted to deduct the amount until the following year.

Moving Expenses

Moving your family and household effects is expensive, especially if you have to foot the bill yourself. Fortunately, help is available in the form of tax deductions for most of your moving expenses. As might be expected, there are a number of catches, but most Canadians moving closer to a new job location will qualify.

To be eligible you must move at least 40 kilometers (25 miles) closer and be employed or begin to carry on a business at a new location. Intracity moves to, for example, a larger home, will not qualify. The move must be within Canada. Students also qualify for moves to begin full-time attendance at a post-secondary institution, and for moves back home to take up summer or full-time employment. At least one of the locations must be in Canada and the 40-kilometre rule applies. Only the student may claim the deduction.

Eligible expenses are deductible only from income earned at the new location. Amounts not deducted in one year may be carried forward to the next year. For example, a student's moving expenses are only deductible by the student from scholarship, bursary and research grant income (not from teaching assistant income) for moves to the post-secondary school location, and only from summer job income for moves back home.

The following moving expenses qualify for the deduction:

- ☐ Travelling costs, including a reasonable amount for meals and lodging, plus meal and lodging costs for up to a total of fifteen days at the new or old location.
- ☐ Moving and storage costs for your household effects.
- ☐ The costs of cancelling a lease or selling the old home (but not including any loss incurred on such a sale. As well, any expenditures to make the home more saleable do not qualify).
- ☐ The legal costs of purchasing a new home, as well as any transfer or registration taxes, but only if a home was sold at the old location.

If your employer reimburses you for any portion of these costs, you may still claim all your moving expenses, but you must include the reimbursement in income. A reimbursement of reasonable costs of moving that are not deductible is not considered a taxable benefit of employment. These include the costs of maintaining an empty house at the old or new location, house hunting expenses, meals and lodging in excess of the fifteen-day limit, child care and even a loss on the sale of your home at the old location.

TAX TIP When transferred to a new location by your employer, it is to your advantage to structure your new remuneration package so that as many moving costs as possible are financed by your employer, either directly or by reimbursement. Reimbursements for many expenses connected with a move are not taxable. On the other hand, if you receive additional salary and deduct your expenses, you may still be out of pocket.

TAX TIP If you receive only a partial, non-taxable reimbursement for your moving expenses, arrange with your employer for these amounts to be allocated to non-deductible expenses of the move.

TAX TIP Since an unexpected tax liability may arise with a move to a higher-rate jurisdiction, you might want to postpone your move until after the year end. Provincial tax is based on your province of residence on December 31. Alternatively, you might consider accelerating your move if you are moving to a province with a significantly lower tax rate.

TAX TIP If your marginal tax rate will increase significantly with a move, for example, from the 17% federal rate to the 26% rate, it may be worthwhile postponing your move so that your moving expenses are applied against income that is taxed at the higher rate and therefore produce a larger tax saving.

Employee Benefits—Taxable or Not?

Employee benefits have become an increasingly important part of the remuneration package of most Canadians. Some of these benefits are taxable (their value is added to your income and appears on your T-4 slip); some are not taxable (see list below); and special rules apply to others—employee loans and stock options are covered separately below, and company cars are discussed in the next chapter.

There are a variety of non-taxable employee benefits paid for, or financed by, an employer. These include:

- ☐ Employee discounts, if available to other employees,
- ☐ Subsidized meals, provided the employee pays no less than the employer's cost for the meal,

- ☐ Use of the employer's recreational facilities, but not including board and lodging,
- ☐ Social or athletic club membership dues, if it is principally to the employer's advantage for the employee to be a member,
- ☐ Moving-expense reimbursements (see above),
- ☐ Group term life insurance, but only up to $25,000 of coverage,
- ☐ Private health services coverage,
- ☐ Reimbursement of convention expenses, if the employee's presence is required for business purposes and this function is the main purpose of the trip,
- ☐ Tuition fees, if the course is taken for the benefit of the employer during normal working hours, with the employee being given time off with pay,
- ☐ Uniforms and special clothing and
- ☐ Employee counselling, if provided in-house, or provided in respect of the employee's physical or mental health, termination of employment or retirement.

You should note that frequent-flier discounts arising from business trips may give rise to a taxable benefit when you use the discounts for personal flying. Employer-funded financial counselling provided by an outside party is also taxable. As well, if your employer helps offset the cost of the purchase of a home computer, even though it is used only for the employer's business, a taxable benefit will arise. If you do not own the home computer, the size of the taxable benefit will depend on how much personal use is made of it.

TAX TIP Don't lose sight of the fact that, if your remuneration is not affected, it is always cheaper for your employer to provide a good or service than to provide it yourself, even though a taxable benefit will arise — the

tax payable on the benefit will always be less than your personal cash outlay.

Employee Loans

If you receive a low-interest or interest-free loan from your employer, you will likely be in receipt of a taxable benefit, although there are a couple of exceptions. But first, the general rule.

Let's assume that your employer lends you $10,000 interest-free for the year. You will be deemed to have received a taxable benefit equal to the difference between the interest actually paid on the loan and the interest that the Government considers should have been paid on the loan. For this purpose, the taxman uses the prescribed interest rate, which is the rate Revenue Canada charges on late tax instalments or pays you if you happen to remit too much tax. This rate is adjusted quarterly and is based on short-term interest rates in the preceding quarter. We will assume that the prescribed rate is 10%, which means that your taxable benefit is $1,000 (10% of $10,000).

If your employer had charged you an interest rate of 6% and you had indeed paid this interest no later than 30 days after the end of the calendar year, your taxable benefit is reduced by the amount of interest actually paid. In this case, you would have paid $600 of interest, and your taxable benefit would be limited to $400 ($1,000 minus $600).

TAX TIP Even though you may be getting a taxable benefit, interest-free or low-interest employee loans are much cheaper than borrowing personally.

For example, let's assume that you receive the $10,000 employee loan interest-free, instead of borrowing commercially at 13%. If your marginal tax rate is 40%, you will pay tax of $400 on the $1,000 taxable benefit, which is the cost of the loan for the year. If you borrowed commercially, your interest cost would be $1,300, or $900 more than the cost of the employee loan.

Several important points should be considered in connection with loans received from employers.

☐ Almost every type of debt that results by virtue of your employment will qualify as an employee loan. These include third-party loans, loans made to family members and even loans made to unrelated parties. Thus, you may not see a penny of the loan, but will be responsible for paying the tax on the benefit.

☐ The employee-loan rules also apply to loans made to shareholders of corporations, whether in their capacity as a shareholder or employee. Additional "shareholder loan" restrictions will apply for loans made because the individual is a shareholder.

☐ If an employee loan is made on a commercial basis (that is, commercial interest rates apply and commercial terms and conditions of the loan are enforced), the employee-loan rules do not apply.

☐ If an employee loan is forgiven, the employee will be in receipt of a taxable benefit equal to the amount involved, less any repayments.

☐ Any taxable benefit included in income in respect of an employee loan qualifies as interest actually paid on the loan. Thus, the amount may be deductible if the proceeds of the loan are used to purchase investments or even to acquire an automobile that is to be used in the employer's business.

TAX TIP **Interest-free employee loans used to acquire investments are tax-free, since the taxable benefit is eliminated by the offsetting interest expense deduction equal to the benefit.**

TAX TIP If you are borrowing for investment reasons, as well as for personal expenditures (which means this interest expense is not deductible), arrange to have any employee loans directed toward the personal borrowing. Your cash outlay will be less as long as the prescribed interest rate is lower than the commercial rate at which you normally borrow.

Home-purchase employee loans are treated slightly differently from regular employee loans. Such a loan must enable the borrower or a related person to acquire a home that the employee will occupy, or to refinance a mortgage on an employee-occupied home. The taxable benefit on this type of loan is calculated using the lesser of the prescribed interest rate in effect at the time the loan was made or renewed, or the current prescribed rate. Such loans are considered to be renewed every five years, which means that the prescribed rate is adjusted accordingly.

TAX TIP If interest rates appear to be on the rise, it may be worthwhile arranging for your employee home purchase loan to be renewed for a further term, but no longer than five years. This lower rate of interest will be locked in and the resulting taxable benefit will remain constant for the period. Because of the way the prescribed rate is calculated, you will know in advance if it will move upward in the next quarter.

If you are acquiring a home and are eligible to claim moving expenses (see above), a deduction is available against any taxable benefit included in income equal to the benefit that would otherwise be incurred on an interest-free home purchase loan of $25,000. For example, assume that you receive a $75,000 home-purchase loan from your employer at 6% and the prescribed rate is 10%. Your taxable benefit would normally be $3,000, calculated as $7,500 (10% of $75,000) minus interest paid of $4,500 (6% on $75,000). However, since you are eligible to claim moving expenses, you may deduct the benefit that would be incurred on a $25,000 interest-free loan from the benefit of $3,000. Thus, your taxable benefit is $500 ($3,000 minus $2,500 – 10% on $25,000).

Note that this reduction in your taxable benefit on a home purchase loan is applicable for no longer than five years.

Employee Stock Options

Stock options can be a lucrative perk of employment—if they are exercised at the right time to minimize tax, and particularly if you work for a successful company whose stock continually increases in value.

There are no tax consequences to being granted a stock option. A tax liability will only arise when you exercise the option, and, in the case of certain private company options, only when you actually sell the shares. The rules for options vary considerably, depending on when the option was granted and if the option qualifies for special treatment.

Unless noted otherwise below, you are subject to a taxable benefit at the time you exercise a stock option equal to the difference between the fair market value of the stock at the time of exercise and the option price. The benefit is included in your employment income and is taxed at full rates. When the time comes to sell the shares, any gain is a capital gain, the cost of the shares being the fair market value at the time you exercised the option.

For example, let's assume that you have been granted an option to purchase shares of your company at $10 each any time before 1995. You exercised the option in 1988 when the fair market value of the shares is $19 and you sell the shares in 1989 for $25. In 1988 you had a taxable benefit of

$9 per share included in your income. In 1989, you have a capital gain on the sale of the shares of $6 each. Two thirds of this, $4 per share, is included in income for tax purposes, although this gain is eligible for your $100,000 capital gains exemption.

TAX TIP **Assuming that the fair market value of your option shares is increasing, the sooner you exercise the option, the smaller your tax bill may eventually be when the shares are sold, since a larger portion will relate to a capital gain. However, by exercising early, you may be prepaying tax, which involves a cost. And don't forget that exercising a stock option is primarily an investment decision, and should not be based exclusively on tax considerations.**

There are two major exceptions to the general rule. First, if the option was granted after February 15, 1984 and three conditions were observed, your taxable benefit will be reduced when you exercise the option. In 1988 and 1989, the benefit is reduced by one third, and in 1990 and following years by one quarter, which essentially accords capital gains treatment to these options. To qualify:

- ☐ The exercise price for the share cannot be less than its fair market value when the option was granted,
- ☐ The employee must deal at arm's length with the corporation and
- ☐ The shares under the option arrangement must be common shares that meet specific criteria.

Using the example above, but assuming the shares meet the above qualifications, you would be entitled to reduce your 1988 taxable benefit of $9 by one third, or by $3 per share. Note that the benefit is based on the difference between the exercise price and the fair market value at the time of exercise, while the reduction will only be available if the exercise price is equal to, or greater than, the fair market value when the option was granted.

TAX TIP Since the benefit reduction slips to one quarter in 1990 for post February 15, 1984 options, consider exercising such options before the end of 1989.

Stock options issued by Canadian-Controlled Private Corporations (CCPCs) are accorded preferential treatment, again assuming certain conditions are met. These options are subject to taxation only when the shares are actually sold. However, you must own the shares for at least two years before you sell them, and you must be dealing at arm's length with the CCPC when you exercise the option. When you dispose of the shares, the difference between the fair market value of the shares at the time the option is exercised and the exercise price is treated as a taxable benefit and is reduced in the same manner as above. The difference between the fair market value and the sale price is a capital gain, eligible for your capital gains exemption. If you exercised the option before May 23, 1985, both the capital gain and the taxable benefit are eligible for your lifetime exemption. When selling shares, those acquired before May 23, 1985, are considered to be sold before those acquired after that date.

Once again, we will use the numbers in the above example, except you will sell the shares in 1991 instead of 1989 so that you meet the requirement of holding on to the shares for at least two years. Your taxable benefit is reduced by one quarter of $9 ($2.25) to $6.75, and the taxable portion of your gain is $4.50 (three quarters of the total gain of $6). However, these taxable amounts, totalling $11.25, are only included in your income in 1991 when you actually sell your shares.

TAX TIP Don't forget that a portion of your capital

gain on CCPC options may be eligible for the additional $400,000 lifetime capital gains exemptions, if the CCPC qualifies as a small business corporation (see Chapter 11).

TAX TIP If you borrow to finance the purchase of shares when exercising stock options, the interest expense on the loan is deductible. However, it will be added to your Cumulative Net Investment Losses (CNILs — see Chapter 11).

TAX TIP If you think that you may be subject to the Alternative Minimum Tax (AMT), you might want to postpone exercising some stock options since these acquisitions may add to your AMT liability.

8
Automobile Expenses

A company car is one of the most common and most attractive "perks" to which the average employee has access. You might use the company car exclusively for business, or primarily for pleasure. You may even own or lease the vehicle yourself, but be reimbursed for expenses or receive a car allowance. No matter what the arrangement, it's always cheaper, and hence an important part of anyone's remuneration package, for your employer to finance automobile costs than to shoulder them personally. However, any personal use of the car financed by your employer will generally result in a taxable benefit being added to your income.

The tax rules that segregate and value the personal use of an automobile have been in flux for a number of years. With tax reform on the law books, perhaps we can now look forward to a few years of stability. Whether the new rules are more fair than the old ones is debatable. They are certainly as complex. The new rules were made law in September, 1988, but took effect nine months earlier on the first of January. Hopefully, you heeded the warnings issued as far back as mid-1987 when tax reform was first released—keep meticulous records of your business kilometres versus your personal ones, as well as all expenses. This should make wading through the rules slightly easier, and it will make it possible for you to derive the maximum benefits from your company car perk.

Employer-provided Cars

If you are provided with a car, you are probably receiving a two-part taxable benefit. The first, called the standby charge, arises simply because you have access to the car and can use it for personal reasons. The second, called the operating expense benefit, arises from operating costs that are borne by your employer, but relate to personal use of the car. Both are reduced by reimbursements you make to your employer.

Generally, these rules, and other automobile tax provisions, relate to passengers cars, which are automotive vehicles designed or adapted primarily to carry passengers and their luggage. Seating capacity must be limited to nine persons, including the driver. Station wagons, vans and pick-up trucks are included in the definition if not used primarily for the transportation of goods and equipment.

Standby Charge Benefit

A standby charge benefit is included in income if your employer, or a taxpayer related to your employer, has supplied you with a car that is available for your personal use, or the personal use of someone related to you. If the employer purchased the car, the standby charge is calculated as:

2% × (cost of the car) × (number of days available for personal use divided by 30)

The number of days divided by 30 is rounded to the nearest whole month, with 0.5 being rounded down. If the car was purchased after June 17, 1987, for more than $20,000, the employer is denied a deduction for associated expenses above the $20,000 limit, but the employee's standby charge will be based on the actual cost of the car.

If your employer leases the car, the benefit is calculated as:

⅔ × (leasing cost that relates to days available for personal use)

The leasing cost does not include expenses that relate to insurance or damage or liability costs. If the car was leased after June 17, 1987, for more than $600 per month, the employer is denied a deduction for the leasing costs above this limit, but the employee's standby charge is based on the actual leasing cost. Since leasing costs for identical cars can vary considerably from dealer to dealer, Revenue Canada has, in effect, placed a ceiling on the value of the car to be leased, which works out to about $23,000 (manufacturer's list price plus sales tax).

TAX TIP **Since the standby charge is based on the number of days the car is available for personal use, try to keep these days to a minimum. For example, if you are on vacation or do not use the car on weekends, leave it at your employer's place of business. And don't forget to subtract the days when the car is in the shop being repaired.**

If the car is driven strictly for business purposes and is not used for driving back and forth from home to work, generally the car will not be available for personal use. If you go directly from home to a customer or another business stop (but not your regular place of employment) at the beginning of the day, or drive from a customer to your home at the end of the day, these trips constitute business, not personal, use.

TAX TIP **The standby charge is calculated on the original cost of the car and does not decline as the value of the car declines with age. After a few years, it may be cheaper to eliminate the standby charge by buying your company car from your employer or the leasing company. Alternatively, your employer could sell the car to a leasing company and then lease it back. The reduced payments will result in a reduced standby charge to you.**

TAX TIP A reduction of the lease payments reduces the standby charge. Thus, increasing the term of the lease could be considered. Tax deductibility, however, effectively limits the term of car leases.

The standby charge is reduced if personal kilometres driven are less than 10% of total kilometres in the year (that is, business use is at least 90%). To determine the reduced amount, you divide your total personal kilometres by 1,000 times the months of availability (as calculated above) and multiply this number by the standby charge already calculated. Confused? Well, let's look at an example. Assume that the car cost $16,000, is available 365 days of the year and personal kilometres total 3,000 out of 42,000 total kilometres. The standby charge would normally be calculated as:

2% × $16,000 × (365/30) =
2% × $16,000 × 12 =
$3,840

The reduced standby charge is calculated as:

3,000 divided by 1,000 × (365/30) =
3,000/12,000 =
¼ or 0.25

This fraction is multiplied by the normal standby charge:

$3,840 × 0.25 = $960

Thus, your standby charge in this instance is only $960. If your personal kilometres were 4,500 instead of 3,000, the standby charge would be $3,840 because personal kilometres exceed 10% of total kilometres (4,500/42,000 = 10.7%).

While the arbitrary nature of the 90% rule may not make much sense, it does make sense to pay close attention to your personal kilometres if you are anywhere near the magic 90% number for business kilometres driven.

TAX TIP Reducing personal kilometres can mean substantial tax savings. To get your personal use below 10%, consider renting a car for a weekend out-of-town trip or taking taxis for those Christmas shopping trips. Of course you will have had to keep accurate records to know how close you are to the 10% threshold.

TAX TIP If you have two cars, one of which is supplied by your employer, reserve your own car for personal use whenever possible.

The standby charge is reduced for persons employed primarily in the selling or leasing of automobiles.

Operating Cost Benefit

A taxable benefit for operating costs is included in your income if your employer pays these costs for your personal use of the car. The amount of the benefit is determined by dividing personal kilometres by total kilometres, and multiplying this fraction by the total operating costs. Alternatively, if the car is used primarily for business (that is, more than 50%), you may elect to use one half the standby charge as the operating cost benefit.

TAX TIP There may be little point in electing to use the simplified method of calculating your operating-cost benefit if business kilometres are well above the 50% figure.

Operating costs for purposes of the operating-cost benefit include all costs directly associated with the operation of the car, such as:

- ☐ Licence and insurance;
- ☐ Car washes;
- ☐ Gasoline, net of any gasoline tax rebate (see below);
- ☐ Service charges, including tune-ups, oil changes and the cost of grease and oil;
- ☐ Minor repairs, including replacing tires, windshields and other parts; and
- ☐ Major repairs, including damages resulting from accidents.

These costs may be capitalized, which increases the cost of the car and therefore your standby charge. In this situation, the capital cost of the car cannot be increased above $20,000.

Expenses not considered as operating costs include interest on loans used to purchase cars and parking costs.

Employee-provided Cars

If you provide your own car to use in your employer's business, you have two primary concerns — are you allowed to deduct your expenses? And will allowances or reimbursements received from your employer be included in your income for tax purposes?

Who Can Deduct Car Expenses?

Generally, if you use your car for business purposes, most expenses are deductible (the clergy also qualify). Slightly different rules apply to salespersons compared with employees in general.

Employees may deduct travelling expenses if:

- ☐ The amounts are reasonable;
- ☐ You carry on the duties of employment away from your employer's office or in different places;
- ☐ You are required under your contract of employment to pay at least some of your own expenses;

☐ You are not given an allowance for expenses that is excluded from income; and
☐ You do not claim the deduction available to salespersons (see below) or to railway or transport company employees.

A salesperson who is an employee may deduct employment-related travelling expenses if:

☐ They are reasonable;
☐ They do not exceed commissions earned;
☐ You are required to pay the expense under a contract of employment;
☐ Your duties of employment are carried on away from the employer's office; and
☐ You are not given an allowance for expenses that is excluded from income.

A salesperson's claim for interest on money borrowed to purchase a car and the depreciation expense on the car is not limited by commissions earned.

Deductible Car Expenses

To determine the deductible amount of your car expenses, the total must be prorated based on business kilometres divided by total kilometres put on the car during the year. You must total up your actual expenses; you are not permitted to use a cents per kilometre calculation. Both fixed and operating expenses are deductible.

Operating expenses include ordinary repairs, gasoline (net of any gasoline tax rebate – see below), oil and grease and servicing charges. Fixed expenses include:

☐ Interest paid in the year on money borrowed to purchase a car;
☐ Depreciation (called capital cost allowance);

- ☐ Insurance and licence fees; and
- ☐ Leasing costs.

However, note that these expenses may be limited in certain circumstances and they must be prorated for business use of the car. In particular:

- ☐ For depreciation purposes, the cost, including provincial sales tax, of a car acquired after June 17, 1987, cannot exceed $20,000.
- ☐ The monthly interest cost on money borrowed to purchase a car after June 17, 1987, cannot exceed $250.
- ☐ For car leases entered into after June 17, 1987, the deductible monthly cost cannot exceed $600.
- ☐ Depreciation (capital cost allowance) cannot exceed 30% of the undepreciated capital cost of the car (15% in the years of acquisition and sale). No adjustments will be allowed to a corporation, trust or partnership if a car with a capital cost in excess of $20,000 acquired after June 17, 1987, is sold and either too much depreciation (recapture of capital cost allowance) or not enough depreciation (terminal loss) has been claimed. No such adjustments are allowed to an individual in respect of any car sold.

Net accident-repair expenses are fully deductible if the automobile was used for business at the time of the accident. No deduction is allowed if the car was being used for personal reasons at that time. Business-related parking expense are fully deductible.

TAX TIP **Even if you have enough cash to pay for a new car, consider borrowing since a large portion of the interest expense could be deductible, depending on your business use of the car.**

TAX TIP **If you borrow from your employer to pur-**

chase a car, remember that any taxable benefit included in income is deductible based on the business use of the car.

Reimbursements and Allowances

Yes, reimbursements and allowances are different, at least for tax purposes. An amount paid to you by your employer that represents what you actually paid out in the course of your employment is a reimbursement. To get it, you must account for the expenses to your employer. An allowance is an amount paid to you for which you do not have to account.

Neither a reimbursement nor an allowance is taxable if it is reasonable and relates to business use of the car. For an allowance to be non-taxable, it also must be based solely on business kilometres put on the car. As well, the employee can receive no other reimbursement, in whole or in part, for the same use of the automobile. Of course, you are not allowed to claim car expenses if you are in receipt of a non-taxable reimbursement or allowance.

TAX TIP If you feel that the reimbursement or allowance does not cover your actual expenses, you may be able to choose to include the reimbursement or allowance in income for tax purposes and claim your actual expenses (contact your District Taxation Office).

You would certainly choose to claim your expenses if you received an allowance that was included in income because it was not reasonable or was based, for example, on time worked, rather than on business kilometres driven.

Gasoline Tax Refund

Included in the price of gasoline is Federal Excise Tax. Generally, if you are eligible to deduct your car expenses, you qualify for a rebate of a portion of the tax paid. Rebates must be applied for on special form XE-8. The amount of your refund either must reduce the amount of your gasoline expenses claimed, or it must be included in income. No refund is available on diesel fuel.

Self-employed Persons and Automobile Expenses

If you are self-employed and own or rent a car to earn income, you may deduct your car expenses. Similarly, if you are a member of a partnership and personally own or rent a car to earn income from the partnership, you may deduct your car expenses, as long as the partnership does not reimburse you for the expenses. The deductibility of amounts is exactly the same as for employees, outlined above under "Deductible Car Expenses". Don't forget that you may be eligible for the gasoline excise tax refund.

If your home is the base of your business operations, expenses incurred in driving from your home to clients are deductible. If you have more than one business location, expenses incurred in travelling between the different premises of that same business are deductible.

Travelling to Rental Properties

If you carry on the business of renting out real estate, the cost of travelling to and from the rented properties is deductible. If you own two or more rental properties, you can deduct car expenses incurred for collecting rents, supervising repairs and generally providing proper management.

If you receive income from only one rental property that is not a business and you personally perform part or all of the necessary repairs and maintenance, the cost of using your car to transport tools and materials is regarded as part of the repair and maintenance expenses of the property, not a travelling expense. Otherwise, car expenses are not deductible from your rental income.

Employer-owned or Employee-owned—Which is better?

Unfortunately there is no definitive answer to this question. It really depends on the amount of business use compared with personal use of the car, your tax rate, your employer's tax rate, the age and cost of the of the car and even the cost of financing. It is just as difficult to answer the buy or lease question.

If you can put some numbers together, you might be able to come up with a very rough answer, which may or may not be particularly reliable. There are a lot of variables to consider. If you think that you are missing out on substantial tax savings or your employer will foot the cost, consider getting professional advice. Remember that there is probably a 50-50 chance that you are doing the right thing now, so the professional's fee could be wasted. The same can't be said for employers seeking advice in this area. Often there are savings to be realized if their automobile policies are reviewed regularly, particularly since the legislation has been changing so often.

Record Keeping

The value of keeping accurate, up-to-date and complete records of your automobile expenses and business kilometres driven cannot be stressed too much. You will likely have to produce the information for your employer in order for taxable benefits to be determined or to collect your allowance or reimbursement. The information is obviously needed to make your own claims for deductible automobile expenses. In fact, it is possible that the tax authorities will at some point want you to back up your claims with detailed records. Disappointing them could mean a disappointing amount of tax could become payable.

9

Tax Planning for the Self-Employed

To those contemplating running their own business (that is, being self-employed), two benefits immediately come to mind — the personal freedom of being your own boss, and the almost unlimited tax deductions you hope will come your way.

More often than not, personal freedom to the self-employed means hard work and a lot more hours spent on their business than they ever put in working for an employer. And although there are certainly a greater variety of tax deductions available to the self-employed, you don't automatically qualify, just because you are "in business". First, you must be running a bona fide business. Second, your expenses must be business-related and be reasonable. More importantly, you may be courting disaster if you lose sight of the fact that a tax deduction does nothing more than reduce your costs. A $40 tax saving on a $100 expense still means an out-of-pocket cost to you of $60 — in no way does the tax deduction eliminate your expense.

Nevertheless, the rewards of running your own business are many, not the least of which may be the monetary rewards from taking advantage of a variety of tax-planning opportunities, a few of which are summarized below. Please note that this chapter only looks at a handful of ideas. Accounting for your business income and expenses, and any related planning, is not dealt with at all. You should also note that the comments below deal with unincorporated businesses. If your business is incorporated or you are thinking of incorporating, you should seek professional advice.

Are You Employed or Self-employed?

This question is not always easy to answer and will depend on your particular circumstances. Often it boils down to how much control your "employer" or major client exercises over your work or services. For example, if the "employer" controls your work hours, requires you to work on his premises and furnishes you with all the equipment, supplies and office help that you need, you likely would still be considered an employee in the eyes of Revenue Canada.

Some employees in senior positions provide their services through a corporation. However, special rules are imposed on these "personal-services" corporations. As a result, there are no significant advantages to this type of arrangement. In fact, you could be paying more tax than necessary if you have set up a "personal services" corporation.

Are You Earning Business Income?

If you are not an employee and you have not formed a corporation through which you will provide your services, you then must determine whether or not you are actually "in business". This is obviously not a problem if you are earning your living from the activity. Income tax law defines a business to include a profession, calling, trade, manufacture or undertaking of any kind whatever, including an adventure or concern in the nature of trade. Bear in mind that an individual can have more than one business, in which case the profits of each must be calculated separately. This is important when income is allocated to two or more provinces, or when the sale of assets results in the recapture of capital cost allowance.

Concerns may arise, however, if you pursue an activity part-time. There are no firm rules to determine whether the activity is a business or a hobby, in which case no deductions for expenses would be allowed and any incidental income generated would not be taxable. However, if you sell an asset acquired in such an activity for proceeds of more than $1,000, any gain may be subject to tax as a capital gain from a personal-use property (see Chapter 11).

Generally, you must have a reasonable expectation of profit from the activity for it to be considered a business, and you must pursue the activity in a manner likely to bring you a profit. You need not produce a profit immediately, or even have a history of making profits; you simply have to "plan" to make a profit and have a reasonable chance of doing so.

If you are a writer, musician, painter or other type of artist, trying to break into the field, it may be difficult to establish that you are pursuing your activity with a profit motive. It can take a number of years before it could be judged that you have a reasonable expectation of earning a profit. Revenue Canada has published detailed guidelines for individuals in this situation in Interpretation Bulletin IT-504, available from your local District Taxation Office.

Choosing a Year-end When Starting Up a Business

A business may end its fiscal year at any time in the year. Generally, fiscal years must be no longer than 53 weeks (most are exactly one year long). However, you are permitted to have a shorter than normal first fiscal year. Once you choose your fiscal year end, you must apply to Revenue Canada to have it changed. There must be some underlying business reason for the change. Revenue Canada will not permit a change if the only reason you made the request was to save tax dollars.

Income earned from the business to the end of the fiscal year is reported in your tax return of that calendar year. For example, if your fiscal year ends on January 31, 1989, you would report your business income in your 1989 tax return which you would file on or before April 30, 1990. If the fiscal year of your business ended on December 31, 1988 – only a month earlier – you would report your business income in your 1988 return, which would have to be filed by April 30, 1989 – a full year earlier.

By ending the first fiscal year of your business sometime after December 31, a significant tax deferral is available. For example, if you start your business in September 1988 and choose a January 1989 year end, the tax payable on income earned in September is not finally due until April 30, 1990, more than a year and a half later.

However, you might be required to pay some tax throughout 1989 by instalments (see Chapter 16), which would then be applied against your final tax bill owing. Therefore, you ought to keep your eye on the amount of taxable income that the business is generating. Generally, you would choose to cut off your first fiscal year at the point where you just begin to pay tax on your income, after allowing for all deductions and tax credits, but you would want this date to be after the end of the year so that you defer your first year's tax liability. Meeting both goals may not be possible, especially if you start your business toward the beginning of the year.

However, if you do meet both goals, no tax will be payable for over two years on the business profits. For example, assume that the income you earn from September 1988 to January 1989 attracts no tax. During calendar 1989, you need not pay tax by instalment (see Chapter 16), since you are not taxable for that year. During calendar 1990, you also are not required to pay tax by instalments because no tax was payable in the previous year. Your first tax instalment is due March 15, 1991, and your 1990 tax bill is not due until April 30, 1991. In this case, the taxman has not received a dime from you for over two and a half years.

TAX TIP **When determining the date on which to end the first fiscal year of your business, crunch your numbers with a tax return in front of you. Your business's first year can end on any day in the month, not just the last day.**

Proper timing of your first year-end may eliminate tax payable altogether in that year, but don't forget that those tax chickens you deferred may come home to roost when you cease to carry on a business and become employed again. In that year, you may feel that you are being taxed twice—once on your business income (most of which may have been earned in the preceding year) and again on your employment income.

If operating losses are incurred in the first few months, it may be advantageous to adopt a fiscal year-end that does end in that first calendar year. These losses then could be used to reduce other income earned in the year or even in any of the preceding three years. Unused losses can be carried forward seven years.

Purchasing Depreciable Assets

You are allowed to claim depreciation (technically called Capital Cost Allowance – CCA) on assets bought for use in the business, such as office equipment, computers and automobiles, as well as the premises out of which you work (if you are the owner) and the improvements you make to the premises (called leaseholds) if you are the tenant. The rate at which you claim depreciation is dictated by tax law.

Generally, in the year you buy an asset, you may claim only half of the amount of CCA to which you would otherwise be entitled. If your fiscal year is shortened for any reason (perhaps it's your first year of operation), your CCA claim is further prorated based on the length of the fiscal period. Since CCA claims are based on the undepreciated cost of the asset at the end of the year, you will not be able to claim CCA in the year that you sell the business asset, unless you continue to own other similar assets that are pooled for CCA purposes with the asset that you sold. Separate CCA pools must be established for each business automobile that you own, as well as each piece of real estate costing over $50,000 on which you claim CCA.

TAX TIP Time the purchase and sale of capital assets properly so that your CCA deductions are maximized.

For example, try to purchase assets before the end of your fiscal year, so that you are at least entitled to that half-year CCA claim. When selling an asset, try to dispose of it after the end of the year, so that you receive a full depreciation claim in the previous year. Generally, you must take delivery of an asset and put it into use to claim CCA in the first year.

Retirement Plans

If you are self-employed, you may only have access to RRSPs to help you with your retirement saving. These are discussed in Chapter 5. Your net income from the business, after expenses, is earned income for purposes of making RRSP contributions.

If you have employees, you might want to consider setting

up a registered pension plan, to which you may belong. However, there may be a significant expense involved. Professional advice should be sought and other alternatives explored.

Office in Your Home

Depending on the nature of your business, you may be affected by the new tax reform rules on home office expenses. No deduction for expenses will be allowed unless the work space is your principal place of business, or is used "exclusively on a regular and continuous basis" for meeting clients. If you operate a full-time business out of your home, you should have no trouble satisfying these conditions. However, if you operate a part-time business or have other office space out of which you conduct your business, you likely will be denied a deduction for office expenses.

As well, a new tax reform rule requires that home office expenses be deducted only from income earned from the business carried out in the home. If these expenses exceed your income from the business, they may not be claimed against other sources of income. However, you may carry the expenses forward to a future year and deduct them when you are finally generating income from the business.

TAX TIP Since the new restrictions apply only to unincorporated businesses, it may be worthwhile incorporating your business to gain access to the larger deductions. The corporation would rent the office space from you, at a reasonable rate.

If you are eligible to claim home-office expenses, you must meet one other important condition. The space set aside for the business (it must be a room or several rooms) must be used exclusively for the business. Setting up your computer and file cabinets at one end of the living room will not entitle you to claim home-office expenses.

Home-office expenses are generally apportioned based on the space used. For example, if you have an eight-room house and use two rooms for your business, two eighths of your home expenses would be deductible. You may also base your claim on square footage of the house used for the business. Utilities, house and contents insurance, property taxes and mortgage interest (not mortgage principal repayments) are deductible. Depreciation on a home that you own is also deductible, but this will interfere with claiming a principal residence exemption on any capital gain eventually realized on the sale of the home. Generally, it will not be to your advantage to claim depreciation, and besides the claim will be relatively small, especially on an older home.

Business Meals and Entertainment Expenses

Even if you are a one-person operation, you are not exempt from the new 80% rule introduced with tax reform on all forms of entertainment and meal expenses. The rule itself is straightforward. Only 80% of eligible expenses incurred are deductible for tax purposes; the other 20% must be borne by the business. Ostensibly, this 20% represents what you would have paid in any case for your own meals and entertainment.

There are, however, several exceptions to this general rule. For example, the 80% limitation does not apply to "incidental beverages and refreshments" (for example, coffee and doughnuts) provided at conferences, seminars, conventions or provided to clients visiting your offices.

TAX TIP Try to bill meal and entertainment expenses directly back to your clients, since these are not subject to the 80% limitation if they are billed to or reimbursed

by an identifiable person and are identified on the appropriate invoice. The client then becomes subject to the 80% limitation.

Automobiles Used in Your Business

These were discussed in detail in the preceding chapter. The rules for self-employed individuals are certainly not as complex as those for employees who are supplied a car by their employers. However, to make the most of automobile claims, you must keep meticulous records of personal and business kilometres driven, as well as all expenses. Remember that self-employed persons claiming a variety of expenses are more likely to be audited by Revenue Canada than employees. Good records are the only way you have of substantiating your claims.

Paying a Salary to Your Spouse or Children

If your spouse or children work for you, you may pay them a salary, as long as the wages are reasonable in relation to the work performed. Any amounts paid are deductible from the income of the business (that is, your income) and are taxable in the hands of the recipient. This can result in substantial tax savings if that income would otherwise have been earned in your hands and be taxed at a high rate (see Chapter 13 on Income Splitting). As well, your spouse and children will be able to contribute to RRSPs, since the wages paid to them represent earned income. And both will be able to contribute to the Canada or Quebec Pension Plans, although your children must be at least eighteen years old.

Husband and Wife Partnerships

If you and your spouse operate the family business together, you should consider setting up a partnership, rather than having one spouse pay a salary to the other. With a partnership, all business income is earned by the partnership and then allocated to the partners on some pre-arranged basis. The criteria used are generally time spent on the business, capital (that is, money or assets) contributed to the business and relevant expertise brought to the business.

For example, if one spouse is a lawyer and the other a legal secretary, it would be very difficult to establish that a 50-50 income allocation of partnership profits is reasonable, since it is likely that the lawyer's expertise would be responsible for generating the bulk of the income. However, a case for a 50-50 split could possibly be made if the secretary half of the partnership was responsible for attracting and maintaining all the business.

TAX TIP If you have decided to form a husband and wife partnership, consider drafting a formal partnership agreement that spells out the duties of each partner, capital contributed and profit allocation, as well as what each partner is expected to contribute if the partnership loses money.

It is important to bear in mind that Revenue Canada has the power to allocate partnership income on a basis that it deems reasonable. Thus, you should plan on keeping records of your respective activities to support your partnership income allocation in case you are challenged.

10
Investment Income

Astute investors never lose sight of the fact that it is the after-tax result of their activities that matters, not the nominal yield on their investments. Tax itself seldom motivates a particular acquisition, but tax can be a crucial factor when deciding among alternative investments with similar yields.

Knowing how investment income is taxed and what impact that tax will have on your own holdings should make you a more astute investor. The better your investing strategies, the more you'll have in your pocket at year end.

Tax reform has reduced the tax on investment income (interest and dividends), but increased the rate on capital gains (see next chapter). In the past, dividends were more lightly taxed than interest, but the spread in tax rates between the two has shrunk dramatically. In theory this should increase the attractiveness of interest-bearing investments compared with those that pay dividends. Of course, the financial market place will have its say. Generally, over the longer term, investments of similar risk should produce approximately the same after-tax return, at least for upper-income investors.

Still, tax is only one element in the investing equation — and in many situations, a minor element. The quality of the investment and security of your invested capital should always be considered ahead of tax. You should also bear in mind that the tax savings that result when you lose your shirt on an investment never make up for your out-of-pocket cost of the investment.

Table 2
Comparative Marginal Tax Rates (Federal)

			Capital Gains	
Tax Bracket	*Interest* %	*Dividends* %	*1988 and 1989* %	*1990 and future years* %
17%	17.51	4.72	11.67	13.13
26%	26.78	16.30	17.85	20.09
29%	29.87	20.17	19.91	22.40

Rates include 3% federal surtax.

Interest Income

Interest income is taxed in the same manner as employment or business income. The full amount is included in income and is taxed at your normal rates. Until the end of 1987, the first $1,000 of Canadian interest and dividends were exempt from tax, but that break disappeared with tax reform. Foreign interest income, including any foreign tax withheld, is also included in income and is taxed in the same manner as Canadian interest. However, if you paid foreign tax on the interest, you may be entitled to a foreign tax credit, which will offset some of the Canadian tax owing.

All types of interest income are taxable, including bank interest (even if you did not receive a T-5 slip from the bank detailing how much interest you earned), Canada Savings Bond interest, interest you receive on a second mortgage that you may have taken back when you sold your last house and even interest earned on a loan you made to your spouse.

Under the three-year accrual rules, you can be taxed on interest you have not received. In some situations, you may even be taxed on interest that you personally did not earn—see Chapter 13 on income splitting.

Three-Year Accrual Rules

It is not possible to defer the receipt of interest (and hence tax on the interest) for any longer than three years, thanks to the three-year accrual provisions in the tax law. These say that income earned on any type of debt obligation, including deferred annuities and certain life-insurance policies, must be reported for tax purposes at least every three years—whether or not you have received that interest. Of course the rules don't apply to interest earned in statutory deferred-income plans such as RRSPs.

These rules took effect in 1982. Deferred-income securities acquired before November 13, 1981, are excluded from the rules as long as they are "locked-in", which essentially means the terms of the security cannot be altered. Income from securities acquired between November 13 and the end of 1981 first had to be reported in 1987.

TAX TIP If you currently hold certain "locked-in" securities with compound interest acquired before November 13, 1981, you may want to hold on to them to avoid paying tax on the related investment income until the contract matures and you actually receive the interest.

The most common types of deferred-income securities are five-year GICs (Guaranteed Investment Certificates), which repay principal and all accumulated interest at the end of the investment period, and compound-interest Canada Savings Bonds, which have the same repayment feature, but a slightly longer term. These kinds of securities are considered to have a December 31 anniversary date. For example, if you purchase a five-year GIC on March 21, 1989, all interest accrued to December 31, 1992, must be reported for tax purposes in your 1992 tax return. When the GIC matures on March 21, 1994, and you actually receive the interest, the remaining interest accrued from January 1, 1993, must be reported in your 1994 tax return.

TAX TIP Canada Savings Bonds should be reviewed every October. Those maturing at the end of the month should be cashed and reinvested promptly at the maturity date. No interest is paid after the maturity date. Similarly, if you own bonds with interest coupons attached, these should be clipped and cashed on the date specified on the coupon. However, if they are dated close to the year end, consider waiting until January to cash the coupon, which defers tax for a year.

TAX TIP Annuities that provide for equal annual or more frequent payments and that commence the payments shortly after the date of purchase are not subject to the three-year accrual rules. In some circumstances, they may offer deferral possibilities, depending on the term of the annuity.

One of the disadvantages of deferred-interest securities is that you must pay the relevant tax, even though you have not received the income. However, you should note that this is a disadvantage only from a cash flow point of view—you may have to rob Peter to pay Paul. You will still be better off from an investment point of view deferring the interest, even though your deferral is limited to three years (almost four years if you purchase the security on January 1).

For example, assume that you have a choice of buying a $1,000 deferred interest five-year GIC, or one that pays interest annually. Your marginal tax rate is 40%. Which one would you be better off with?

The deferred-interest GIC is your best bet, despite the fact that you must pay tax on the interest accrued at the end of three years and have not actually received any income. Assuming that the GIC pays interest at the rate of 10% compounded annually, and all funds can be reinvested at this rate, you will be about $12 better off with the deferred-interest GIC if your marginal tax rate is 40%. Why? Because interest is being earned on interest before tax is applied with the first GIC, at least for the first three years. With the second GIC, your after-tax rate of return each year is only 6%. Of course, when deciding between the investments, you should consider other investment factors, such as whether interest rates are likely to rise.

The three-year accrual rule is not inflexible. You have the option of reporting your deferred-interest income each year. You must elect whether or not to report the interest on each such security. For example, you might elect to report your compound-interest Canada Savings Bond (CSB) interest each year rather than every three years, but not elect to do so on your five-year GICs. When your CSB matures, the election expires and does not apply to the next compound interest Canada Savings Bond you buy. It also does not apply to other CSBs that you may buy while you own the particular compound interest bond.

TAX TIP Consider electing to report interest income from particular securities annually if it is likely that the three-year accrual rules will propel you into a higher tax bracket.

Using the 1988 tax brackets outlined in Chapter 2, assume that your taxable income is $25,500 each year. Every third year you must report $6,000 of interest income. Thus, every third year, your taxable income shoots up to $31,500 ($6,000 plus $25,500). Income below $27,500 is taxed at 26%, but the $4,000 you earn above this threshold is taxed at 40%. If you made the election and included $2,000 of interest in income each year, tax would always be paid at 26%, since your taxable income would not rise above the $27,500 threshold. You are prepaying tax two out of every three years, but the tax saving more than offsets any cost associated with the prepayment.

Note that this may not be the case if reporting the accrued interest propels you into the top tax bracket from the middle bracket. There is only a five percentage point difference between the two, which may not produce enough of a tax saving to offset the cost of prepaying tax.

Life Insurance Policies

Accrued investment income on certain life insurance policies purchased after December 1, 1982, is subject to the three-year accrual rules if the amount accumulated by the insurer is above a specified limit (for example, policies paid for by a single premium). Investment income on policies purchased before December 1, 1982, will be taxed only when the policyholder receives proceeds — perhaps as a result of surrendering the policy or taking out a loan under it.

TAX TIP If you are considering replacing a pre-December 2, 1982, life insurance policy, bear in mind that the old policy may receive more favourable tax treatment than the new one.

Canadian Dividends

As noted above, Canadian dividends are taxed more lightly than interest income. But also note that this favourable treatment only applies to *Canadian* dividends. Foreign dividends are taxed exactly the same as interest income, but you will generally receive credit for any foreign taxes paid that can be applied against your Canadian tax owing.

The dividend tax credit acts to reduce the tax on dividends, but how it does this is somewhat complicated. An example will help explain how the tax credit works and why the "taxable amount" of a dividend that you see on a T-5 information slip is more than the cash amount that you actually received.

Let's assume that you receive a $100 cash dividend from ABC Corp., which is a Canadian company. You are in the middle tax bracket (federal tax rate of 26% and assumed provincial rate of 55% of the federal rate). To simplify the example, we'll assume that there are no surtaxes. The dividend must be "grossed-up" by 25% (this is simply the term used to increase the dividend to its taxable amount). Federal tax is calculated and then the dividend tax credit is applied against this tax. Provincial tax is then calculated on the reduced amount.

Cash Dividend	$100.00
Gross-up (25% of cash amount)	25.00
Taxable amount of dividend (from your T-5 slip)	$125.00
Federal tax on $125 @ 26%	$ 32.50
Less dividend tax credit (16⅔% of cash amount of dividend)	16.67
Federal tax	15.83
Add provincial tax @ 55% of federal tax	8.71
Total federal and provincial tax	$ 24.54

Thus, for each $100 of Canadian dividend income you earn, your after-tax return is approximately $75. Compare this with earning interest income that is tax at about 40%, leaving you with only $60 for every $100 earned.

TAX TIP Consider transferring your spouse's Canadian dividends to your tax return. In some situations, the tax savings may amount to several hundred dollars.

You are permitted to include your spouse's Canadian dividends in your income if, by so doing, you will increase your married-status tax credit. *All* of your spouse's dividends must be transferred. You cannot pick and choose in order to maximize the tax savings. Why will this be beneficial? Because the tax savings that result from increasing your married-status tax credit more than offset the extra tax that you must pay on the dividends.

Of course, you should ensure that this will indeed be the case before you formalize it on your return. Generally, if each dollar of dividends transferred results in the restoration of a portion of your married-status tax credit, you will be better off, no matter what tax bracket you are in. However, if the transfer results in your spouse's income falling below the $500 (1988) threshold where you are entitled to the full married-status credit in any case, there may be no benefit. Similarly, if your spouse's income including the dividends is above the personal tax credit threshold of $6,000 (1988) and only a small portion of the married-status tax credit is restored, you may derive no advantage from the transfer.

Shareholders who receive dividends from closely held private Canadian corporations are also eligible for the dividend tax credit. In fact, in 1988, you can receive about $22,000 of dividends and pay no tax, as long as this is your only source of income subject to tax. This isn't as strange as it sounds because, of course, tax is first paid by the corporation before dividends are distributed. It is important to determine the appropriate mix of salary and dividends that you are to receive from the corporation in order to minimize taxes and accomplish your other personal and financial goals. Generally this is done just before the calendar year end. Your accountant or tax adviser will help you come up with the best numbers.

Is It Deductible?—Making Your Interest Expense Inexpensive

Tax reform did not eliminate deductible interest. However, it certainly muddied the investment waters for those claiming the $100,000 lifetime capital gains exemption.

Any interest paid on funds borrowed to earn investment or business income is deductible for tax purposes. That's the general rule. However, there are a number of corollaries to the rule that manage to trip up thousands of taxpayers every year.

Investment income includes interest and dividends, as well as certain other sources of income, such as royalties and "passive" rental income. Technically, investment income does not include capital gains that may be realized on capital properties (see next chapter). However, since many investments, including shares and mutual funds, have the possibility of paying dividends or earning income at some point in time, if they do not currently, interest is generally deductible when such securities are acquired.

TAX TIP If you are buying Canada Savings Bonds on the payroll savings plan, don't forget to claim a deduction for interest expense. Essentially you have purchased the bonds at the first of November with borrowed funds and you repay the loan with interest during the year.

To claim a deduction for interest expense, you do not necessarily have to realize or earn a profit on your investment. You simply have to have a reasonable expectation of profit. Thus, if you realize a loss or do not earn interest or dividends for several years, the deductibility of your interest expense should not be in jeopardy. However, you must have a reasonable expectation of earning more than the amount you are paying in interest. For example, if you borrow at 12% to buy a 10% GIC, you have no reasonable expectation of profit, and a portion of your interest expense will be denied as a tax deduction.

TAX TIP Ensuring that your investment loans are fully documented could save you a headache later on. If your deductible interest is questioned by the tax authorities, they will want to see proof that you actually borrowed the funds, paid the interest, acquired the appropriate investment and retained it during the period you deducted the interest expense.

Your interest remains deductible only as long as you continue to own the investment that you purchased with the borrowed funds. If you sell your investment but do not repay the loan, any interest accruing from that date is no longer deductible. However, if you purchase new securities with the proceeds of sale, all your interest expense will remain deductible as long as at least the original amount of the loan is reinvested. Unfortunately, this will not always be the case. For example, suppose that you originally borrowed $8,000, but your investment turned sour and you sell it for $6,000. You reinvest these proceeds immediately. Now, only 75% of your interest expense is deductible — the ratio of the reinvested amount ($6,000) to the original loan ($8,000).

Tax reform introduced the concept of Cumulative Net Investment Losses (CNILs), which, while not affecting the deductibility of your interest, will certainly add to the paperwork associated with your investing activities. Essentially, the CNIL rules say that the amount you may claim under your lifetime capital gains exemption in any year is reduced by the amount that your cumulative investment expenses, which include interest expense and certain other tax shelter losses, exceed your cumulative interest and dividend income. CNILs are explained in more detail in the next chapter, but you should be aware that there could be a price to pay for the deductibility of your interest.

The interest that you pay on borrowed funds that are used for personal purposes is not deductible. Such borrowing includes personal loans used for vacations or other living expenses, a loan that enables you to purchase the family car and a mortgage that enables you to buy your home or a seasonal residence, used strictly by you and your family. Interest is also not deductible if you borrow to make RRSP or pension-plan contributions, to purchase life insurance, to pay your taxes or to reloan the money to family members. If the transaction is purely capital in nature, such as the purchase of vacant land, again the interest expenses are not deductible. However, the interest is added to the cost of the investment, which reduces your gain on the eventual sale.

TAX TIP If you must borrow, always borrow for investment or business purposes before you borrow for personal purposes. And don't forget the corollary. When repaying debt, always repay non-deductible loans before you repay those on which the interest is deductible.

TAX TIP If you run or are involved in a business, you should always borrow for business purposes, and use your cash on hand to invest. Interest on business loans is deductible, but it does not enter into the CNIL calculations. Thus, you should have much more flexibility to use your lifetime capital gains exemption during the year.

If you have a line of credit that you use both for investment and personal purposes, you might instruct the lending institution to apply all your repayments of principal to the portion of the loan used for personal purposes. Assuming that the bank agrees, you will consequently repay all your personal borrowing before you begin to repay your investment borrowing. The portion of your interest expense on the loan that is deductible will increase rapidly as you reduce the personal portion of the loan, and hence your tax saving will increase. Of course, you could simplify matters by having two loans, one personal and one investment, and arrange with your bank to repay the personal one first.

This is only one technique to reduce your non-deductible debt or convert it into deductible debt.

TAX TIP Consider selling certain of your investments to generate the cash to repay your non-deductible debt. The result should put more cash in your pocket and possibly enable you to borrow more effectively—that is, borrow so that your interest is deductible for tax purposes.

An example will demonstrate how good an "investment" repaying non-deductible debt can be. Assume that you have borrowed $10,000 to purchase the family car. Interest on the loan is payable at 12%. You also have $10,000 worth of Canada Savings Bonds that are paying 9%. To simplify the explanation, we'll assume that no principal is repaid on the car loan in the first year. Only non-deductible interest of $1,200 is paid. You receive $900 of interest on the Canada Savings Bonds, but must pay tax at your marginal rate of 40%. This leaves you with only $540 to apply against the interest expense on the car loan. Thus, you have to dig into your pocket for another $660 to meet the $1,200 interest payment on the loan.

If you simply cashed in the Canada Savings Bonds to provide the funds to purchase the car, you would not earn the $540 in after-tax interest, but you also would not be paying the $1,200 interest to the bank. Therefore, you would be better off by the $660.

Of course, the bank will still likely loan you $10,000 if you still need it. This time, however, you would use the proceeds of the loan for investment purposes. The interest would now be deductible.

There are two possible snags in this technique, neither of which should discourage you from pursuing it. Recent court cases have pronounced against a series of transactions undertaken only to reduce taxes. And tax reform has introduced new rules, called the General Anti Avoidance Rules (GAAR), which may prohibit such transactions. A taxpayer's ability to substitute deductible debt for non-deductible debt through a series of transactions has also been questioned. This commonly happens when a taxpayer sells investments, uses the proceeds to repay a mortgage on their home, remortgages the home and uses the proceeds of the mortgage to repurchase the investments or similar investments. The argument goes that, if the lure of substantial tax deductions for the mortgage interest did not exist, the taxpayer would have had no intention of selling the original investments.

We think it unlikely that GAAR will be applied against individuals, unless there is some wide-spread type of flagrant abuse of tax law. We also recommend that you not replace investments with the exact ones sold to eliminate the non-deductible debt. In fact, you may run into other tax problems if any of these investments are sold at a loss and subsequently repurchased (see Chapter 11).

Investment Holding Companies

In the past, individuals formed investment holding companies (basically a corporation that holds your investment portfolio) for three primary reasons:

- ☐ The tax savings that resulted from flowing investment income through the corporation and the tax deferrals if investment income was left in the corporation;
- ☐ Income splitting (see Chapter 13), which permitted other family members to earn investment income and usually be taxed at lower rates;
- ☐ Estate planning, which allowed the major shareholder of the corporation to deal with assets on death more effectively and reduce taxes that could be owing.

The third item above still applies if you have, or are considering setting up, an investment holding company. However, income splitting through an investment corporation was effectively eliminated by laws introduced in 1986 and 1987, although arrangements in place before October 28, 1986, are still valid. Tax reform has done some damage to the tax-saving possibilities. In fact, beginning in 1988, there may be a tax cost, albeit a relatively insignificant one, associated with flowing income through an investment holding corporation, whether the corporation earns interest, dividends, capital gains or other types of investment income. However, some tax-deferral advantages may still exist.

TAX TIP If portfolio share investments are held by an investment holding corporation and the dividends are not immediately flowed through to the shareholders, a significant tax-deferral advantage may result. The size depends on your province of residence, but may be as high as $8 for every $100 of dividends received.

Because the lifetime $100,000 capital gains exemption is not available to corporations, any capital gains realized by an investment holding corporation will be taxable. As well, you should bear in mind that the additional small business corporation capital gains exemptions of $400,000 does not apply to shares of investment holding corporations.

TAX TIP If you have an investment holding corporation or plan to establish one, ensure that you and other family members will realize sufficient capital gains personally to utilize your respective capital gains exemptions. You might consider selling your investments to the corporation so that you personally realize the capital gains.

While there are costs associated with maintaining an investment holding corporation, there are also costs associated with dismantling one, which may be significant enough to offset the minor tax costs of flowing income through the company. In view of the potential income-splitting and estate-planning benefits, you might want to maintain the corporate structure.

It is beyond the scope of this book to explain in detail the taxation of investment holding companies and how investment income is flowed through to shareholders. Briefly, interest and the taxable portion of capital gains are taxed at full corporate rates, which are somewhat lower than personal rates. A special refundable tax is levied on dividends received by the corporation, unless the company owns at least 10% of the dividend-paying shares. The investment holding company flows income through to shareholders by paying its own dividends. These trigger a refund of the refundable tax to the investment holding company. The dividend tax credit acts to reduce your personal tax payable on the dividends received from the investment holding company. The tax-free portion of a capital gain is distributed by means of a non-taxable *capital* dividend to shareholders of the investment holding company.

If you have an investment holding company established and you plan to purchase, or already own, a vacation property in the United States, there may be some advantage in arranging for the corporation to own the property. You should seek professional advice in this area. In fact, you may want to have a professional tax adviser review your investment holding company to ensure it is still cost effective and that there are not other, less costly methods of accomplishing your financial goals.

11
Capital Gains

With the introduction of tax reform last year, the taxation of capital gains has changed significantly. While tax rates have gone down, the effective rate of tax on capital gains has actually increased, and it will go up further. However, the lifetime $100,000 capital gains exemption, which first appeared in 1985, means that most average Canadians won't be paying "too much" tax on capital gains over the next few years.

Yet you just might be paying some tax, even if you are eligible for the exemption. What the Government gives with one hand, it often takes away with the other. The new Cumulative Net Investment Loss rules (CNIL) may limit the amount of the exemption you may claim in any one year, if you claim certain rental losses or borrow to invest or acquire tax shelters.

Taxation of Capital Gains and Losses

In 1988 and 1989, two thirds of any capital gain realized is subject to tax (only 50% was taxable in previous years). This fraction increases to three quarters in 1990 and following years. The taxable amount is included in your income reported in your tax return and is taxed at the same rates as employment or business income. Capital gains or losses are realized only when you actually dispose of a property. The word "dispose" is used because in certain situations you may be subject to rules under which you are *deemed* to have sold a capital property. Most commonly, this occurs when you permanently emigrate from Canada, and it generally occurs on death, although other "deemed disposition" situations may arise if your affairs are complicated.

Table 3

Marginal Tax Rates on Capital Gains (Federal)

Tax Bracket	*1988* %	*1989* %	*1990* %
17%	11.67	11.67	13.13
26%	17.85	17.85	20.09
29%	19.91	19.91	22.40

Rates include 3% federal surtax.

Note that "property" is simply the tax term for all assets of a capital nature. The term is not restricted to real estate. It includes shares in corporations or an interest in a partnership, depreciable property such as cars or machinery or a building, rights or options to purchase or sell property of any kind and even personal property such as antiques, books or boats. Special rules apply in a number of cases (these are discussed later in the chapter) and some dispositions are not taxable. You can even opt for some transactions to be considered income rather than capital in nature, so that the capital gains rules do not apply.

TAX TIP Consider realizing capital gains before the end of 1989. The tax burden increases by about three and a half percentage points in 1990. Bearing in mind other investment considerations, the tax saving is substantial

and may even pay for your brokerage fees on the sale of publicly traded shares.

Capital losses are reduced by the same two thirds and three quarters fractions to determine the taxable amount, called your allowable capital loss. Any allowable losses realized in the year must first be used to reduce all capital gains realized in the year. Any balance remaining can then be carried back to the three immediately preceding years to reduce taxable capital gains, and if any amount remains unused, it can be carried forward indefinitely and likewise be used to reduce capital gains.

Losses carried back and used to reduce capital gains of prior years may restore a portion of your capital gains exemption previously used. For example, assume that you had a taxable gain in 1988 of $5,000, which was exempt under your lifetime exemption. If you carry a 1989 taxable loss of $5,000 back to 1988, there will be no immediate tax benefit, but you will restore $5,000 of your lifetime exemption, which then can be used in future years.

Losses carried forward will be adjusted if necessary to correspond to the appropriate inclusion fraction. For example, the taxable amount of a loss incurred in 1989 is two thirds of the total loss. If it is carried forward to 1990 and used in that year, the taxable amount of the loss will be adjusted to three quarters of the total loss.

Losses that have been carried forward from years before 1985 and remain unused are subject to the old rules, under which up to $2,000 of the allowable loss can be used to reduce income from any other source.

Lifetime Capital Gains Exemption

The lifetime exemption was first introduced in 1985 and slated to be phased in through to 1990 to a maximum of

$500,000. Tax reform capped the exemption at $100,000, but allows the owners of qualifying small businesses and farms an additional exemption of $400,000 when they sell their operations.

The exemption is available to individuals on almost all capital gains, whether realized in Canada or not. Corporations and trusts do not qualify, although capital gains flowed out to beneficiaries from a trust are eligible for the exemption. You must be a Canadian resident to claim the exemption. If you were a resident in Canada only part of the year, you may still claim the exemption if you were a resident of Canada throughout the immediately preceding year or the following year. The exemption is not available when a pre-1985 capital gains reserve is brought into income (see below).

The capital gains exemption available to you in any year is reduced by the amount of any allowable business investment losses and allowable capital losses from other years that you claim in that particular year (see below). As well, an exemption claimed in the year is reduced by any CNIL that you have accumulated. CNILs are explained more fully later in the chapter.

TAX TIP Each family member is entitled to his or her own capital gains exemption. You may want to begin a program to rearrange ownership of capital properties to multiply the exemption. Income splitting is discussed in detail in Chapter 13.

TAX TIP If you are selling United States residential property, the lifetime exemption will apply to any gain you may realize. However, U.S. tax may apply, in which case you will ordinarily be entitled to a Canadian foreign tax credit. You may not be able to claim both the exemption and the foreign tax credit. In many cases, it may be

better not to claim the exemption and apply the foreign tax credit against Canadian tax owing.

The fact that the tax rate on capital gains is increasing as of January 1, 1990, will not affect your access to the capital gains exemption. The $100,000 amount refers to the total gains realized, or taxable gains to a maximum of $66,666.67 in 1988 and 1989, and taxable gains to a maximum of $75,000 in 1990 and following years.

New tax laws are introduced virtually every year, and old laws disappear almost as regularly. In view of the possibility of the capital gains exemption disappearing as abruptly as it was introduced, you should give careful consideration to using the exemption as quickly as you can. Owners of small businesses and farms should be especially concerned with the possible disappearance of the additional $400,000 exemption to which they now may be entitled. This is not say that you should dump all of your capital properties tomorrow. But bearing in mind normal investment considerations, you should review all your holdings, including vacation homes that have accrued gains. You can always trigger capital gains and keep the assets in the family by selling them to other family members.

TAX TIP If you have realized foreign capital gains and are entitled to a foreign tax credit in respect of them, consider carefully how much of your capital gains exemption to claim so that you use up all your available foreign tax credits.

$500,000 Capital Gains Exemption

The $500,000 exemption for small businesses and farmers ($400,000 plus the general $100,000 exemption) is available only for qualifying property. For small business owners, the gain can only be realized on the disposition of shares in an

SBC (Small Business Corporation), provided that the company is an SBC at the time of the disposition and the shares were not held by anyone other than the taxpayer or a related person (generally a member of your immediate family) throughout the immediately preceding 24 months. An SBC is generally defined as a Canadian-Controlled Private Corporation (CCPC) that uses all or substantially all its assets in an active business carried on primarily in Canada. Included are CCPCs whose assets are shares in qualifying SBCs.

TAX TIP **If the shares in your small business corporation have substantial accrued capital gains, you may elect to sell some of the shares to your spouse at fair market value, which triggers a capital gain. Up to $500,000 of the gain could be exempt. Professional advice is a must.**

TAX TIP **The allowable portion of losses realized on the disposition of shares or debt in an SBC may qualify as business investment losses and therefore may be offset against income from all sources (see below). Unfortunately, any such claims for post-1984 losses reduce your capital gains exemption.**

A farm property qualifying for the additional $400,000 exemption can also be operated as a corporation or a farm partnership. The property must be actively farmed by the taxpayer or family members immediately before the sale to qualify for the exemption, and all or substantially all the assets of the business must be devoted to farming.

TAX TIP **Eligible farm property can be transferred to your children at your cost, so there are no immediate adverse tax consequences. However, if you are not going to otherwise use your additional $400,000, you should elect to transfer the property at a higher value and claim the exemption. This "steps up" your child's cost base for**

the farm, and he or she will be liable for a much smaller capital gain on any eventual sale.

Cumulative Net Investment Losses (CNIL)

The CNIL rules were introduced with tax reform to prevent investors from taking a second helping from the tax break menu—a deduction for interest expense as well as a capital gains exemption claim. Beginning in 1988, you must have sufficient investment income (primarily interest and dividends) to offset your deductible interest expense; otherwise, your capital gains exemption claims will be reduced by the amount in your CNIL account.

As might be expected, taxpayers are going to face difficulties when they try putting the rule into practice, for two main reasons. One, investment losses include a variety of expenses besides interest expense, all associated with tax shelters. It may take a bit of effort to sort out the CNIL variety. And two, the offset applies on a cumulative basis—any CNIL not "used" in one year is carried forward to the next. An example will best explain these complex new rules.

At the beginning of 1988, you borrowed $10,000 to invest in a mutual fund. By December 31, you paid $1,300 of interest, all of which was deductible. You still owned your mutual fund investment and you earned $400 of Canada Savings Bond interest during the year. Your CNIL at the end of 1988 is $900—interest expense of $1,300 minus investment income of $400. This $900 CNIL is carried forward to the following year.

In 1989, you again pay interest of $1,300 and earn $400 interest on your CSBs. You also sell your mutual fund investment at the end of the year and realize a capital gain, the taxable portion of which is $1,600. Before attempting to claim a capital gains exemption, you determine your CNIL for the year. Once again, it is $900 ($1,300 minus $400) to which you must add last year's $900 CNIL for a total CNIL of $1,800.

Now, you must offset any capital gains exemption claim by your cumulative CNIL. Since your CNIL ($1,800) is greater than your exemption claim ($1,600), you may not claim an exemption for the gain. The taxable portion of the gain must be included in income and is subject to tax in the normal manner. Your CNIL is reduced by the capital gains exemption claim disallowed ($1,600), so you now have a CNIL of only $200, which is carried forward to 1990.

Three points should be noted. First, your interest expense, plus your other eligible investment expenses and losses, remain deductible. The CNIL rule in no way affects the deductibility of these investment expenses. Second, your eligible capital gains exemption is not reduced by the portion disallowed as a result of the offsetting CNIL; use of it is simply delayed. If your full $100,000 exemption were available when you attempted to make a claim, but were denied by a CNIL, the full $100,000 would still be available in 1990. Third, if you have used up your lifetime capital gains exemption, you are not affected by the CNIL rules — they only apply to persons attempting to claim an exemption.

Investment expenses for a year will generally consist of the following items that are deducted in computing income:

- ☐ Interest and carrying charges relating to investments that yield interest, dividends and rent.
- ☐ Interest and carrying charges relating to an interest in a partnership where the individual is not actively engaged in the business.
- ☐ An individual's share of a loss in any such partnership.
- ☐ One half of an individual's share of deductions attributed to a resource flow-through share or relating to Canadian

exploration and other resource expenses of a partnership arrangement, where the individual is not actively engaged in the business.

- ☐ Any loss for the year from property or from renting or leasing rental property owned by an individual or partnership.

Investment income for a year will consist of the following items included in computing income for the year:

- ☐ Interest, the taxable amount of dividends and other income from investments.
- ☐ The share of income from a partnership where the individual is not actively engaged in the business.
- ☐ Income from property or from the renting or leasing of rental property owned by the individual or partnership.
- ☐ 50% of an individual's share of amounts included in income relating to the recovery of exploration and development expenses.

TAX TIP **You should review your income-splitting arrangements (see Chapter 13) to ensure that neither you nor family members will have CNIL problems of any duration. It may be possible to restructure borrowing or the ownership of some investments to eliminate CNILs any of you may have accumulated.**

TAX TIP **If you have accumulated CNILs and you own deferred-interest securities (see previous chapter), you ought to consider electing to recognize the accrued interest income annually, rather than every three years. This interest income will be applied against your investment losses and will in turn reduce your CNIL, enabling you to use more of your capital gains exemption.**

Trading on Capital or Income Account

Every purchase and sale of a capital asset does not automatically mean that you are entitled to capital gains treatment when you file your tax return. In fact, some taxpayers may prefer "income" treatment, and a group of others have no choice but to report all capital transactions on income account, not on capital account.

If you report on capital account, you are accorded capital gains treatment; that is, only two thirds of the gain is taxed (three quarters in 1990 and following years), capital losses offset capital gains and you may be able to claim your lifetime capital gains exemption. If you report on income account, you are considered to be in the business of buying and selling the particular capital properties. For example, if you are in the real-estate business, your dealings in land may be on income account. If you are a stock broker, your dealings in securities may be on income account, but any land purchase you make may be on capital account. The entire amount of a gain reported on income account is included in income reported for tax purposes, while the entire amount of a loss is deductible from all sources of income, just as if you were engaged in any other type of business.

The advantage of reporting on capital account is that only two thirds of your gain (three quarters in 1990 and following years) is subject to tax. However, your losses can only be used to reduce gains. By reporting on income account, the entire amount of your gains is taxable, but losses are fully deductible against all sources of income. You may elect to have all gains and losses on the purchase and sale of Canadian securities to be reported on capital account. Canadian securities include shares, bonds and other obligations of public and private companies, including mutual fund shares.

TAX TIP Consider making the capital gains election if

you are becoming a more active trader in Canadian securities and you do not foresee any significant losses in the future. The election is made on Form T123, which is available from your district taxation office.

Note that once you make the election, it is irrevocable. All future gains and losses on Canadian securities must be reported on capital account. Traders or dealers in securities, non-residents and certain corporations are not permitted to make the election.

Generally, there is no point in making the election unless you anticipate becoming an active trader or speculator and holding on to your securities only for very short periods of time. You probably have been reporting regularly on capital account and have not encountered any problems. If you have not made the election, the time may come when you have had a series of losses and can make a case for reporting on income account, which may entitle you to deduct the losses from other sources of income.

Commodity and Option Trading

Reaching a decision on whether to report commodity gains and losses on capital or income account may not be easy. Capital gains are taxed less heavily than income gains, but income losses can be used to reduce other sources of income while capital losses can only be used to reduce capital gains. More importantly, interest on loans used to finance your commodity or options transactions will only be deductible if you are reporting gains and losses on income account. This may be the deciding factor. Whichever method you choose must be used consistently from year to year. You cannot switch to income account one year just because you have realized losses and then go back to capital account.

You must report gains and losses on income account for a

particular commodity if you have special information or if you use that commodity in your line of business. You also may have no choice but to report on capital account if you trade infrequently.

Special treatment is afforded commodity straddles, a situation where you take opposite positions on the same commodity. By year end, one position would usually show a gain and the other a loss. An old planning technique involved closing out one position before the end of the year, depending on your particular situation. For example, if you had already recognized capital gains, you might close out the losing side of the straddle to reduce your gains. The other position with the gain would be closed out early in the following year. Any such gain or loss is now denied until both sides of the straddle are closed out.

T-Bills, Strips and other Discounted Securities

When you buy a 90-day T-Bill, you purchase it at a discount from its face value, which is payable on maturity. The difference between your purchase price and its face value is based on current interest rates. It is also the interest that you earn on the security. However, if you sell the T-Bill or other discounted security before maturity, you may realize a capital gain or loss. For example, if interest rates decline after you purchase the T-Bill, its value will increase. If you sell it, a portion of this increase in value will be a capital gain. This same principle applies to interest coupons stripped from government bonds. It also applies to the bond itself.

TAX TIP If you are participating in the T-Bill or stripped-bond markets, don't blindly report all your gains as interest. By calculating the interest and capital components of each sale, you may save yourself a few tax dollars. If you are lucky, your broker will do it for you.

Special Rules for Capital Gains and Losses

Various rules affect how you report your capital gains and losses. Careful observance of these rules could save you hundreds of dollars when it comes time to file your tax return.

Identical properties. When you acquire securities that are exactly the same, say shares of ABC Corp., the shares are pooled for purposes of determining your cost when it comes time to sell a portion of your holdings. For example, if you buy 200 shares today at $5 each (total cost of $1,000) and 100 shares tomorrow at $8 each (total cost of $800), your cost of each share for tax purposes is $6 (300 shares at a total cost of $1,800). If the 200 shares you bought today are sold for $7 a share, you will have a capital gain of $200 ($7 minus cost of $6 times 200 shares), even though you bought these shares for $5 each. If you sell the remaining shares for $10 each, your capital gain will be $400 ($10 minus cost of $6 times 100 shares), even though you paid $8 for each share.

TAX TIP When determining which of your losers to sell before year end, ensure that you have indeed accrued losses on the specific securities, and that you will not be tripped up by the identical properties rules.

Pre-1972 Capital Properties. Before 1972, capital gains were not subject to tax. Thus, if you acquired a property before 1972 and you still own it, the portion of any gain accruing to December 31, 1971, is not subject to tax. To determine the portion of the total post-1971 capital gain, you either must know the value of the property on V-Day (Valuation Day—December 31, 1971) or you may have to have the property valued as of that date, which could run into some expense. There is a published list of valuation-day values for publicly traded securities. If you own identical properties, some of which were acquired before 1972, on disposition you will be deemed to have sold your pre-1972 properties before you sell the ones acquired after 1971.

TAX TIP Before going to the expense of having a property evaluated for purposes of determining the non-taxable pre-1972 gain, ensure that the cost of the valuation will be more than offset by the expected tax saving.

Settlement Date. Transactions involving publicly traded securities take place at "settlement date": five days after the trading date in the case of Canadian stock exchanges.

TAX TIP Don't undermine your tax-planning strategy by ignoring settlement date. In 1988, December 21 (1989 —December 20) may be the last day on which a sale can be considered executed through a Canadian stock exchange in order to be considered a 1988 (1989) transaction. Check with your broker if foreign exchanges have a different settlement date.

If you are trading privately, you have until December 31 to complete the deal. This would occur, for example, if you are selling shares in a private corporation to another shareholder, or selling publicly traded shares to your spouse, as long as the transaction is completed before the end of the year.

Superficial Losses. If you have realized capital gains during the year that are taxable, you may be tempted to sell some of your losers to offset the gain. This is perfectly legitimate, as long as you do not purchase and continue to own the identical security within 30 days before or after the original sale. Otherwise the superficial-loss rules come into play. As well, you cannot arrange for your spouse or a corporation that you control to purchase the identical security.

If you do run afoul of the superficial-loss rules, you will

be denied any loss realized on the original sale, and the amount of the loss will simply be added to the cost of the newly acquired identical security. For example, if you bought 100 shares of ABC Corp. for $10 each and sell them for $6, you will have a loss of $400. But suppose that a few days later you repurchase the shares for $7 each and still own them 31 days after the original sale. Your loss of $400 will be denied and this $400 is added to the cost of the shares you now own, bringing their cost to $11 each.

TAX TIP If you are selling capital properties with accrued losses for tax purposes, but you actually want to continue to own them, wait for at least 31 days to repurchase the securities. Otherwise the superficial-loss rules will deny the loss.

If you have an income-splitting program with your spouse, you may be able to make the superficial-loss rules work to your benefit (See Chapter 13).

Capital Losses Not Allowed. There are two specific situations where you are not permitted to recognize a loss:

- ☐ The sale of capital properties to a corporation controlled by you or your spouse – the property will be considered to be transferred to the corporation at your cost.
- ☐ The sale of capital property to your RRSP or RRIF (or an RRSP or RRIF of your spouse) – the loss is denied in this case entirely. You are much better off selling the property at arm's length and making a cash contribution to your RRSP.

Sales or transfers of property to your spouse are considered to be made at cost unless you specifically elect in your tax return for the transaction to take place at fair market value. You will not be permitted to recognize the loss unless your spouse disposes of the property within 30 days. Sales or transfers to anyone else, including children under the age of 18, take place at fair market value for tax purposes, even though you may arrange for the sale to take place at a nominal value.

Foreign Currency. If your business does not involve foreign currency transactions, you are allowed to realize foreign-exchanges gains or losses of up to $200 a year, before they must be recognized as capital gains or losses. Such gains are reported for tax purposes only when actually realized. The gains or losses can also be reported on income account as long as you consistently use one method or the other.

TAX TIP If you tend to use foreign currencies fairly often, consider setting up a bank or brokerage account in the foreign currency. You will avoid recognizing capital gains and losses, although you may lose out if the Canadian dollar appreciates in value in relation to the particular foreign currencies.

Personal Use Property. Personal use property is any asset that is used primarily for your own enjoyment and would not be considered an investment asset. No losses are permitted on the sale of personal use property, but two thirds or three quarters of gains may be taxable if the property is sold for more than $1,000 using the capital gains rules. Cost for tax purposes is considered to be $1,000. It is a rare case when gains are realized on the sale of personal property sold for more than $1,000.

Listed Personal Property — Art work, Jewellery, etc. Listed personal property is defined as any print, etching, drawing, painting, sculpture or other similar work of art, jewellery, rare folio, manuscript or book, and stamps and coins. The taxable portion of listed personal property gains and losses is the same as that for capital gains and losses. Losses from the sale of listed personal property may be used only to offset gains from the disposition of such property. Such losses may be carried forward for seven years and back three years.

Capital Gains Reserves

If you sell a capital property at a profit and do not receive the full proceeds at the time of sale or before the end of the calendar year, you may be eligible to claim a reserve. What this means is that you report the full taxable capital gain in your tax return and then reduce the taxable gain by the amount of the reserve claimed. The reserve essentially represents the proportion of the proceeds of sale that are not due until sometime after the end of the year. This most often happens when you take back a note payable or perhaps a mortgage for a portion of the proceeds.

However, tax on your gain can be postponed for no longer than five years on most types of capital property. An example will explain the mechanism. Suppose that you sell your vacation property for $100,000 in 1989. You purchased it for $40,000, so you have a $60,000 capital gain. You receive a $25,000 downpayment and take back a mortgage that will be repaid in equal instalments of $15,000 plus interest over the next five years.

The reserve rules state that you must recognize for tax purposes the greater of one fifth of the capital gain in the year of sale or your capital gain times the proportion of the proceeds actually received. In other words, your reserve can be no larger than four fifths of the gain. One fifth of your capital gain is $12,000 (1/5 of $60,000), but you received a $25,000 downpayment in 1989, or one quarter of the total proceeds. Therefore, you must recognize $15,000 in 1989

(¼ of $60,000). The taxable portion in 1989 is $10,000 (⅔ of $15,000).

In the year after the sale your reserve can be no greater than three fifths of the capital gain, that is, you must have recognized at least two fifths of the gain in the first two years. This amounts to $24,000 (2/5 of $60,000). By the end of the second year you have received proceeds of $40,000, which is also two fifths of the total sale price of $100,000. Thus, since you recognized $15,000 in 1989, you need only recognize $9,000 in 1990. The taxable portion in that year is $6,750 (¾ of $9,000).

In 1991, you receive another $15,000 on the note. You might expect to recognize only $9,000 of your gain (15% of $60,000), but the reserve rules state that at least three fifths of your gain must be reported by the end of the third year. Thus, even though you have not received the appropriate proceeds from the sale of the vacation home, you must recognize another $12,000 of capital gains in 1991. The taxable portion is $9,000 (¾ of $12,000). Similarly, $12,000 must be recognized in each of 1992 and 1993, by which time you have reported the entire $60,000 capital gain, even though $15,000 is still outstanding on the mortgage.

Several points should be noted:

- ☐ By not recognizing the entire gain in 1989, a large portion of it becomes taxable at the higher rate that takes effect beginning in 1990, because three quarters of gains will then be taxable.
- ☐ The five-year reserve mechanism is extended to ten years if you are selling qualified farm property or shares in a small business corporation to your children, grandchildren or great grandchildren.
- ☐ If you sold a property before November 12, 1981, and

proceeds are still outstanding, the old reserve rules, which do not limit your reserve claims to five or ten years, apply.

- ☐ For property sold after 1984, any gain recognized under the reserve provisions is eligible for your capital gains exemption.

TAX TIP You might be better off claiming a reserve, assuming that you are eligible, than claiming the capital gain under your exemption. As the gain is brought into income under the reserve mechanism, you may claim the exemption if you have not used up your $100,000 limit.

For example, assume that you realize a capital gain of $100,000 in 1989 and you know that you will realize capital gains in 1990. You have the full amount of your lifetime exemption available in 1989. You have a choice of either claiming the full $100,000 exemption in 1989, which means that no future gains will be exempt, or claiming a reserve in 1989 and using only $20,000 of your exemption. By opting for the second choice, up to $80,000 of capital gains realized in 1990 could be exempt, and tax on at least some of the $100,000 gain is deferred to 1993. If you claim the full exemption in 1989, you will be taxable on all gains realized in 1990, with no deferral opportunities. Bear in mind, though, that gains arising in 1988 or 1989, but recognized in 1990 and future years under the reserve provisions, will be taxable at the higher 1990 rate if they are not eligible for your lifetime capital gains exemption.

Gains on farm property and small business corporation shares that are brought into income for tax purposes under the reserve provisions are eligible for the additional $400,000 capital gains exemption.

Business Investment Losses

Losses incurred on the sale of shares or debt in a qualifying Small Business Corporation (SBC) are treated differently from ordinary capital losses. An SBC is generally defined as a Canadian-Controlled Private Corporation (CCPC) that uses all or substantially all its assets in an active business carried on primarily in Canada. Included are CCPCs whose assets are shares in qualifying SBCs.

The allowable portion of the loss (called an Allowable Business Investment Loss—ABIL) is calculated in the same manner as a capital loss: two thirds is eligible in 1988 and 1989, and three quarters is allowed in 1990 and following years. An ABIL may be used to reduce all sources of income, unlike a capital loss that may be used only to reduce capital gains. Any portion of an ABIL not used may be carried back three years and forward seven years, exactly the same as normal business losses. After that time, business investment losses revert to ordinary capital losses.

Bear in mind that:

- ☐ The sale must be made to an arm's-length party, or on the bankruptcy of the corporation.
- ☐ The business investment loss may be reduced by dividends paid after 1971, if the shares were owned before 1972.
- ☐ Any ABILs realized will reduce your $100,000 lifetime capital gains exemption and your additional $400,000 exemption, in that order.

TAX TIP You should try to delay realizing ABILs until you have exhausted your capital gains exemption. However, bear in mind that by delaying the recognition of an ABIL, you are prepaying tax, which could involve a significant cost.

12
Tax Shelters

Tax shelters aren't what they used to be. Gone are those heady days when you could plunk $1,000 down on a high-risk investment in frontier oil and gas exploration and get more than $1,000 in tax savings—the perfect way to convert a high-risk investment to a no-risk one. Also gone are those investments where you could put up a few dollars, collect your very generous tax savings, and if you were so "lucky", perhaps pay off your outstanding debt with income from the investment. Or perhaps you wouldn't pay off the debt at all.

Over the past few years, the federal government has cracked down hard on tax shelters by tightening up the law and eliminating a variety of incentives. However, the entire financial community has always been one step ahead of our legislators in devising tax-effective investment plans. And legislation, by its very nature, is imperfect. By necessity, it usually paints with a broad brush and demands to be interpreted in specific situations.

Tax reform has hammered a few more nails into the tax shelter coffin, but the beast is certainly not ready for burial. Tax shelters simply will no longer provide the tax benefits that were once available. Now, more than ever before, you should evaluate the investment potential of a tax shelter in the same way as you would evaluate any other investment. Consider the risk involved, the rate of return, the resale potential, the security of your capital and finally the tax consequences. Tax savings should not be the only motivating factor that prompts you to buy the investment.

TAX TIP It's been said thousands of times, but it still bears repeating. It does not make any economic sense to invest in a shelter if there is little chance of either earning income on your investment, or recovering the net amount that you have invested after allowing for the tax benefits.

Methods of Investing

Generally, you will invest in a tax shelter either directly as an individual or perhaps as a joint venturer along with other investors, or indirectly as a limited partner or purchaser of "flow-through" shares. With any of these methods, the benefits of the tax shelter are aimed directly at the individual and are designed to reduce his or her personal tax liability.

As an individual "direct" investor, you acquire a direct interest in the tax-shelter property, usually real estate or other type of rental property, a hobby farm or an off-shore shelter. As a direct owner you are liable for related debts and any actions taken against the owners of the property, a major disadvantage of direct ownership. Liability for debts may be reduced by transferring your interest in the property to a corporation that you or other family members control after the tax benefits have been realized. The major advantage of direct ownership is that you can exercise some degree of control over management of the investment property. In some situations, it may also be easier to dispose of a property that you own directly, compared with trying to sell an indirect interest in a shelter.

As an indirect investor in a limited partnership arrangement, your liability extends only to the amount invested or committed to the partnership. The general or operating partner, often an entity created by the promoter, assumes general liability. Profits, losses and related tax benefits flow through the partnership to the individual investor. An investor's tax benefits are limited to the amount that is "at-risk" at the end of the year, which is generally the cost of the investment for tax purposes, plus partnership income allocated to the investor, minus amounts owing by the investor and amounts guaranteed to flow through to the investor, whether or not the shelter generates any income. For most investments, this means that the tax benefits in at least the first year are limited to the amount of cash actually invested.

Flow-through share arrangements are somewhat similar to limited partnerships. Usually the promoter, which is a corporation, issues the flow-through shares to the investors. The corporation then renounces all the related costs and tax benefits in favour of the investors. These costs and benefits cannot exceed the amount paid for the shares. You are deemed to acquire flow-through shares at a zero cost base so that the entire amount received when the shares are sold will be a capital gain. Once again, your liability is limited to the amount paid for the shares and amounts committed for payment. Generally, investors will find that their flow-through shares are easier to sell than other tax-shelter investments; in fact, some are even listed on stock exchanges.

TAX TIP Every tax-shelter arrangement is complex, although the prospectus issued by shelters offered to the public does try to explain the tax consequences of investing. You are urged to read the prospectus and accompanying literature carefully, compare the shelter with others and then have an independent professional review your choices. He or she will explain exactly what effects the shelter will have on your personal financial situation if it proves to be a winner or a loser.

You should bear in mind that some shelters are structured to take advantage of the lifetime capital gains exemption. If you have used up your full $100,000, the shelter may not prove to be very attractive to you, especially if capital gains are not realized until 1990 or later when three quarters of any gain must be included in income for tax purposes. Also bear in mind that the various deductions, credits and losses from a shelter are generally added to your CNIL account (Cumulative Net Investment Losses) and consequently may reduce your ability to claim the capital gains exemption. As well, an investment in a tax shelter may expose you to Alternative Minimum Tax problems (AMT), and therefore postpone, and perhaps even reduce or eliminate, any tax benefits that you expected from the shelter. These are all good reasons why you should get competent professional advice before investing.

Resource Shelters

Over the last few years, most resource shelters have been structured as flow-through share arrangements. A variety of deductions and credits have been available, all of which flowed-through directly to investors. These included Canadian Exploration Expense (CEE—100% deductible), Canadian Development Expense (CDE—30% deductible on the declining balance basis), Canadian Oil and Gas Property Expense (COGPE—10% deductible on the declining balance basis), capital cost allowance (depreciation) on certain equipment, Investment Tax Credits (ITCs—at various rates) and the Mining Exploration Depletion Allowance (MEDA — 33½% of CEE, fully deductible but only up to 25% of the investor's income).

Several of these incentives are being phased out or reduced by 1990. However, in 1988, the Government announced a new grant program, the Canadian Exploration Incentive Program (CEIP), which provides grants of 30% on up to $10-million a year of eligible expenses incurred by qualified companies that finance grassroots mineral exploration and oil and gas exploration by issuing flow-through shares. These grants can be flowed-through to investors. It appears that the tax benefits of flow-through share investments may still be relatively attractive to top-rate taxpayers, despite the Government's overhaul.

R & D (Research and Development) Shelters

In the past, research and development shelters were structured as limited partnerships. However, with the restrictions placed on limited partnerships, the R & D tax-shelter investing market slowed down noticeably. Nevertheless, the market is expected to revive with new products based on new incentives, since there is a strong feeling in Canada that we should be performing much more R & D, rather than relying on foreign developments.

Perhaps as a result of the adverse publicity given to the Scientific Research Tax Credit (SRTC) program and its questionable "quick-flips", R & D shelter partnerships did not emerge from tax reform unscathed. Limited partners will not enjoy R & D investment tax credits earned by the partnership and their share of partnership losses will be computed before any deduction for R & D expenditures.

Film and Video Shelters

Film and video shelters have lost much of their popularity over the past few years, and could disappear, now that tax reform has implemented new depreciation rules. Before 1988, you were allowed to deduct 100% of the cost of your investment (Capital Cost Allowance (CCA), or depreciation) in the year of investing and the following year. Beginning in 1988, your annual deduction for CCA is limited to 30% on the declining balance basis. However, you will be permitted to claim additional CCA up to the lesser of the undepreciated capital cost of certified film productions and the income (net of expenses and the basic 30% allowance) from all certified productions in the year. The result is that existing film income flows can be sheltered by new acquisitions. As well, the province of Quebec has enriched its incentives for film and video productions undertaken in the province, allowing a 166 ⅔% write-off for qualifying investments.

Lately, video investments have been the big winners, particularly those investing in children's programs. The pay TV explosion has opened up new and profitable markets. Now, more than ever, you must evaluate the viability of the film or video being produced. The income generated by a successful television series could quickly make the astute investor forget the elimination of the 100% CCA rule.

Real Estate Shelters and Other Rental Properties

Real estate has, over the decades, proved to be the most reliable investment one can make. Lately, it has been very profitable in a number of urban centres where home and commercial prices have been skyrocketing. However, no longer can it be considered a good "tax shelter" investment. Very few up-front or "soft" costs are immediately deductible upon making the investment. The CCA rate has been reduced to 4% declining balance on all buildings, and CCA claims cannot be used to create or increase a loss. Finally, one has to wonder if the real-estate market in late 1988 has become overheated and is poised for a shake out. Not to be ignored either is the threat of higher interest rates over the next year or two, perhaps adding greatly to the cost of a real-estate investment.

Other rental property shelters operated as a business face the same problems. These include hotels, restaurants, nursing homes and even shipping containers. As well, many promoters were structuring the acquisition of personal property, such as yachts, houseboats and motor homes, as tax shelters. The boat or vehicle would then be chartered out most of the year. CCA claims on these kinds of recreational property cannot be used to create or increase losses, seriously reducing the tax benefits of the investment.

Farm Shelters

The attraction of a farm shelter lies primarily in the possibility of being able to claim losses against other sources of income. The most common operation of this sort is the raising of race or show horses, although any "farming" operation will qualify, including market gardening, flower growing for the wholesale market and even raising an exotic type of animal for food.

The key to a farm shelter is the business aspect. You must have a reasonable expectation of eventually earning a profit from the farming operation. If farming is not at the centre of your livelihood, but is carried on as a sideline business, your ability to claim losses is restricted in a year to $2,500 plus half of the next $12,500 of losses ($5,000 before 1989). Unused losses can be carried forward to future years. The unused half may be applied only against farm income in future years.

Farmers may use the cash basis of reporting income, which means that cash outlays for expenses, including the purchase of inventory, are deductible immediately and income is recognized only when it is actually received. Since start-up costs for a farming operation are usually significant, this means that large deductions may be available in the first few years, if you are not classified as a part-time farmer. However, tax reform introduces a mandatory inventory adjustment in respect of purchased inventories on hand in years when cash-basis accounting shows a farm loss. This acts to reduce your losses. As well, reasonable salaries may be paid to family members for work performed on the farm, and the interest expense on funds borrowed to purchase the farm is deductible and does not form part of your CNIL. Finally, eligible farm property may be transferred to your children without incurring any liability for tax on capital gains.

If you run your farm strictly as a hobby with no reasonable expectation of profit, Revenue Canada considers that you are not operating a business, in which case you are not allowed to claim any farm-related deductions from income for tax purposes.

Provincial Shelters

A number of provinces operate venture capital programs that encourage investments in small and medium-sized businesses. Generally, individuals (and in some cases corporate investors) receive generous grants or credits against provincial tax payable if the appropriate investments are made.

Several provinces also have instituted stock savings programs for individuals making investments in public companies that reside in the province. The incentive takes the form of a credit against provincial tax payable or a deduction from income.

Off-shore Shelters

It is extremely difficult to shelter income from tax by investing in another country. First, Canadian tax applies to your world-wide income, not just income earned in Canada. Thus, earning non-taxable amounts in a tax haven does not excuse you from paying Canadian tax on the income. Second, shelter arrangements designed to avoid Canadian tax have, since 1986, been caught by a rule that requires you to report income on such an investment for tax purposes, whether you have actually earned any income or not. The amount is computed by applying the prescribed rate of interest as set by the Government to the cost of the investment.

You may also want to bear in mind that Revenue Canada has several "information sharing" arrangements in place with other jurisdictions. You might want to glance at Chapter 16 to review the penalties that can be imposed for wilfully evading tax.

13
Income Splitting with Family Members

For many households, income splitting is an effective way to reduce the family's total tax bill each year. Depending on the size of your income and the thoroughness of your income-splitting program, the tax savings can be significant—perhaps as much as several thousand dollars each year.

However, getting on the income-splitting bandwagon has become much more difficult in recent years with the Government's crackdown on virtually any tax-planning idea that threatens the Federal Treasury. Income splitting is a highly visible, often sought-out target. Please take note that the opportunities discussed in this chapter, and of course those discussed in other chapters, are based on the law in effect at press time—September 1988. If you are considering some of the more complicated income-splitting ideas, you are cautioned to check with your professional adviser before implementing them. The law and Government policy are in constant flux. There is no guarantee that the planning you choose to put into action will still be sanctioned a year or even a few months from now.

What Is Income Splitting?

Income splitting is having income that normally would be taxed in the hands of the highest-income family member taxed at lower rates in the hands of a lower-income family member. Tax may even be eliminated if the family member has very little or no income. The value is obvious. If you earn income that is taxed at the top marginal rate of 45%, but you can arrange for your spouse to earn it so that it is taxed at the lowest marginal rate of 26%, your family has just saved $19 in tax for every $100 of income earned.

There is a limit to how much tax you can save each year by splitting income with your spouse—about $6,800 at current rates. This is the maximum tax saving that could result if one spouse earns no income and some of the income of the higher tax-rate spouse were taxed in the hands of the lower-rate spouse. Few couples are so fortunate as to be concerned with this limit; most will be content with saving a few hundred dollars a year, which can be done relatively easily.

Worries

Many taxpayers are worried about transferring assets and the resulting income to their spouse, primarily because of the possibility of divorce. For income splitting to be effective, the transfer must be irrevocable; that is, the spouse becomes the owner of the asset and you lose control over it, unless you place the asset in a carefully structured trust (see below). The new family-law regimes that are now in place in most provinces make this worry largely academic. On divorce, family assets and in several provinces, all assets acquired during the marriage will be split. If that is the case in the province where you live, there is no point in forgoing perhaps thousands of dollars in tax savings. Family law has become extremely complex over the past few years. Legal advice in this area is a must.

Other taxpayers can't see the point of splitting a few thousand dollars of income if their married-status tax credit will be reduced. They comment, "doesn't the tax cost offset any tax saving?" The answer is a simple no. For example, if you are in the top tax bracket, your marginal rate is 45%. If that income is transferred to your spouse, he or she may pay no tax, but your married-status tax credit will be reduced accordingly (actually your spouse can earn up to $500 in 1988 with no effect on the credit). However, the credit is reduced only at the rate of $26 for each $100 your spouse earns. In other words, the income that was being taxed at 45% is now effectively being taxed at 26%. That's a $19 tax saving on $100 of, for example, interest income.

The Attribution Rules

As noted above, income splitting has come under attack by the Government. A variety of rules have been in place for decades to discourage income splitting. However, the tax-planning community had devised a number of ways to side-step these regulations and to achieve the desired income-splitting goals. So recently, the Government has added a host of new provisions to the lawbooks.

Essentially the rules say that if you transfer assets to your spouse or a child under eighteen years of age, in virtually any manner whatsoever, directly or indirectly, the investment income (including interest, dividends, rental income, etc.) will be taxed in your hands and not in the hands of your spouse or child. As well, capital gains or losses realized by your spouse on the sale of transferred property will be attributed to you. Attribution of capital gains does not apply on transfers to children. The most recent addition to the attribution rules sees low-interest or interest-free loans to any family member, whether under or over eighteen, being snared, if one of the main reasons for the loan was to reduce or avoid tax.

These rules will be explained in more detail as we examine various income-splitting opportunities, but you should be aware that a great variety of transactions are caught by the attribution rules: loans, loan guarantees, transfers through trusts or corporations, gifts, sales and even third-party arrangements. The law is complex and comprehensive. And if several pages of legalese in the Income Tax Act are not enough, Revenue Canada can resort to its GAAR provisions (General Anti-Avoidance Rules) to put a stop to income-splitting schemes our legislators have not anticipated.

But this doesn't mean that there are still not a variety of ways to split income with family members. There are a number of exceptions to the rules; certain types of income are not covered; and some income splitting is even sanctioned by the law. For example, business income is not attributed. Neither is income that results if a loan is made that bears interest at commercial rates or the prescribed rate, and the interest is actually paid within 30 days of the year end. Similarly, sales to a spouse at fair market value are not caught, if you receive adequate consideration in return.

You should note that the attribution rules cease on divorce and on the death of the transferor. They also cease when the transferor becomes a non-resident of Canada. For most transfers to minor children, the rules cease to apply in the year the child turns eighteen.

Techniques for Splitting Income with Your Spouse

Most of the techniques outlined below are easy to implement and cannot be attacked under the attribution of tax-avoidance rules. However, several might be termed aggressive, in which case you ought to seek professional advice before implementation.

TAX TIP Instead of using funds for investing, the higher-income spouse should pay all family expenses while the lower-income spouse invests as much of his or her income as possible. Eventually, the lower-income

spouse's income will escalate to the point where it is more or less equal to that of the higher-income spouse.

When putting this technique to work, you should try to keep your income and your spouse's completely segregated. There will then be no question as to who really owns the investments and is responsible for reporting the investment income. You should apply the segregation rule to all sources of funds, including inheritances or insurance proceeds the lower-income spouse may receive, money brought into the marriage and child tax credits received as a tax refund.

TAX TIP If cash gifts are expected to be received from relatives, these should be made to the lower-income spouse who could then invest the cash and generate investment income that would be taxable in his or her hands.

Giving cash is distasteful to many, but the tax savings can add up if you and your relatives make this a habit. Explaining the lack of "real" gifts to your children is another matter entirely.

TAX TIP The higher-income spouse should try to pay the lower-income spouse's taxes. This will only be possible if the lower-income spouse pays all or a portion of his or her taxes by instalment.

TAX TIP The higher-income spouse might consider giving the lower-income spouse cash to pay the interest on loans.

With both these ideas, you would give your spouse cash that does not directly or indirectly generate income that could be attributed back to you, at least according to the income tax rules. If you attempt to pay off the principal on any loans your spouse has outstanding, and not just the interest owing, you will run afoul of the attribution rules, if the proceeds of the loan have been used to generate investment income or capital gains.

TAX TIP The higher-income spouse should consider making the payment on insurance carried by the lower-income spouse. This would apply to many types of insurance. However, if the policy contains an identifiable investment element, the attribution rules may apply.

TAX TIP The higher-income spouse should consider paying off the lower-income spouse's personal debts, such as those on credit cards. As long as the amount borrowed was not used by the spouse to generate investment income, the attribution rules will not apply.

You should be aware of the substituted-property rules, which essentially say that the attribution rules will apply if the spouse sells a non-income producing asset originally acquired with funds loaned or transferred by the other spouse and buys an investment property with the proceeds.

TAX TIP The higher-income spouse might consider giving or lending the lower-income spouse funds or assets, even if the attribution rules will apply. In short order, the lower-income spouse will begin to earn "interest on interest", which is not attributable.

Historically, the attribution rules have not applied to income earned by the lower-income spouse on income already attributed to the higher-income spouse—that is, interest on interest. This income belongs to the lower-income spouse and is taxed in his or her hands. For example, if your spouse earns interest income of $5,000 that is attributed to you, the income that your spouse earns on that $5,000 next year is taxed in his or her hands. The question is, how much of a difference will this make in a couple's tax position?

As might be expected, it depends on how much is transferred to the lower-income spouse and what the rate of return is. However, if your spouse earns interest at 10% on $50,000 that you would otherwise earn, he or she will be reporting over $1,000 of interest for tax purposes by the third year after the transfer. Each year, of course, you will still report the $5,000 earned on the original $50,000.

TAX TIP Where possible, the higher-income spouse should claim deductions on his or her tax return, while the lower-income spouse would claim tax credits. The deductions are worth more to the spouse with the higher marginal rate of tax, while the tax credits increase the size of the lower-income spouse's after-tax income that would be available for investing.

It is only possible to do this in limited situations, but every little bit helps. For example, the lower-income spouse might report all the family's charitable donations, political contributions and medical expenses that generate tax credits, while the higher-income spouse would pay and report deductible items like those for safe-deposit fees, investment management or investment counsel fees.

TAX TIP If one spouse pays the non-household expenses of the other, for example, school expenses, these should be structured as a loan. Later, if the "educated" spouse becomes the higher-income earner, the loan can be repaid to the lower-income spouse and the proceeds invested to generate additional income for that spouse.

As with many of the more complicated income-splitting techniques, this one must be carefully documented and the respective income of the spouses must be segregated.

TAX TIP Consider making a spousal RRSP contribu-

tion if you expect your spouse's income to be considerably lower than yours on retirement. Spousal RRSPs are discussed in Chapter 5.

TAX TIP If you are near retirement, consider splitting your Canada/Quebec Pension Plan (C/QPP) benefits. You can opt to have C/QPP cheques made payable to both you and your spouse so that your spouse then reports half your C/QPP benefits for tax purposes. This would only be worthwhile if one of you is taxed at a higher marginal rate than the other.

TAX TIP If you are planning to sell property to your spouse, and don't want the attribution rules to apply with respect to any resulting income your spouse might earn, be sure to abide by the tax rules. Most importantly, you must sell the assets at fair market value and receive property of at least the same value from your spouse.

Normally, the transfer of an asset to one's spouse is made at cost, so no gain or loss results on the transfer. However, you may elect in your tax return (a letter explaining the situation will do) to sell property to your spouse at fair market value (FMV). As a result, you must recognize any gain or loss for tax purposes in the year of sale. If you wish the attribution rules to no longer apply, you must recognize the gain or loss for tax purposes and you must receive consideration from your spouse equal to the FMV of the property you sell. This can take the form of money, other property (if there is any doubt about value, get both assets professionally appraised) or a loan payable by your spouse. Such a loan must be bona fide, with reasonable repayment terms. It must carry a reasonable interest rate—either the commercial rate at the time the loan was made, or interest at the prescribed rate at that time. Interest must actually be paid by the spouse within 30 days of the end of each year during which the loan is outstanding; otherwise the attribution rules will apply.

TAX TIP You might consider arranging for the higher-income spouse to purchase assets owned by the lower-income spouse. The sale would take place at fair market value and the lower-income spouse would then have extra cash to invest.

This planning would work if the spouse inherited the asset or brought it into the marriage. A wife's jewellery inherited from family members is often the subject of this kind of transaction. Whether the asset sold is jewellery, an antique or a race horse, the seller of the asset can certainly continue to use it.

TAX TIP Instead of one spouse selling the other an asset for cash, you might consider swapping assets of equal value in a bona fide sales transaction.

For example, you might think of swapping your ownership interest in the family cottage to your spouse in exchange for assets he or she has inherited or acquired with his or her own cash. When the cottage is eventually sold, all or a portion of the capital gain will be recognized by your spouse, perhaps acting to reduce tax payable. Don't forget that your spouse has his or her own $100,000 lifetime capital gains exemption.

TAX TIP If you would like to sell a capital asset to your spouse, but he or she would not have the income to pay the interest on a loan, consider selling your spouse an option to purchase the asset, which would be exercised at some future point when it has increased in value and your spouse is prepared to sell the asset.

An example will help explain how the option to purchase technique works. Let's assume that you own a rare coin that you bought for $1,000 and is now worth $4,000. You sell your spouse an option to purchase the coin for its current fair market value of $4,000. The option agreement states that the option must be exercised within, say, ten years; otherwise the option expires. Your spouse pays you $300 for the option, which is fair market value for this type of option (you should determine this at the same time you get the coin appraised to determine current fair market value).

Five years later, the coin has appreciated significantly in value. Your spouse exercises the option and immediately sells the coin for $11,000. Out of the proceeds, he or she pays you the option price of $4,000. Your spouse now has a capital gain of $6,700 (sale price of $11,000 minus option price of $4,000 minus cost of option of $300). Don't forget that you must include the option premium of $300 in your income for tax purposes in the year you granted the option, and your capital gain of $3,000 (option price of $4,000 minus your cost of $1,000) is reported in the year your spouse exercises the option. There is no attribution of the capital gain realized by your spouse, because you sold the coin at fair market value of $4,000 by granting the option, and you received equal consideration ($4,000) from your spouse when the option was exercised.

TAX TIP Don't forget that the attribution rules also apply to capital losses. If you have realized capital gains that are taxable and your spouse owns securities with accrued losses that he or she plans to sell, you can make the superficial loss rules (see Chapter 11) work to your benefit.

For example, assume that your spouse purchased shares for $7,000 but they are now worth $3,000. Your spouse sells the shares for $3,000 and you purchase the identical shares within 30 days. Your spouse is not allowed to recognize the

$4,000 loss, and you are considered to have purchased the shares for $7,000, the cost of the shares to your spouse. If you hold on to the shares for more than 30 days and then sell them, you will be allowed to recognize any loss for tax purposes, which then could be used to reduce any capital gains that you have realized in the year.

TAX TIP If your spouse has borrowed on his or her own account to finance the acquisition of property that will eventually produce capital gains, consider giving or lending funds to your spouse to pay off the loan. Any resulting capital gain will not be caught by the attribution rules, although income earned on the borrowed funds will be attributed after the loan is paid off.

Note that you cannot have guaranteed your spouse's bank loan, since this would be caught by the attribution rules at the time the loan was made.

TAX TIP Even if the lower-income spouse pays interest on a spousal loan, a significant benefit will arise over the long term if the amount of investment income earned is greater than the interest paid on the loan.

This tip seems self-evident, but is actually ignored by many couples. Let's look at a typical example. If the prescribed interest rate stands at 9%, your spouse should be able to earn 10% or 11%, and perhaps more if he or she takes on some additional risk. The interest paid is deductible in the spouse's hands, perhaps almost eliminating any tax on the interest income. You will be better off including interest at 9% in income than interest at 10% or 11%. And eventually, your spouse will begin to earn interest on interest which will not be attributable.

The prescribed rate is usually lower than commercial rates, so this is the rate to use on a loan. You can let the interest rate float with changes in the prescribed rate, for example, if interest rates were stable or declining. Or you can set a specific term for the loan and use the prescribed interest rate in effect at the time you set the particular term. Because of the way the prescribed rate is calculated, you know a month or two in advance if it is going to go up a point or two. This allows you to lock in a specific term at the lower rate.

TAX TIP If the higher-income spouse has lent funds to the lower-income spouse, don't set up a monthly payment schedule for the interest. Wait until just before the statutory deadline — 30 days after the year end before making a commitment. Depending on the performance of the investments acquired by the lower-income spouse, you can then decide whether the interest should be paid or the securities sold and the loan repaid.

For example, if the lower-income spouse's investments have generated sufficient interest or dividends to finance the interest payment, it may be worthwhile paying the interest and keeping the loan intact. On the other hand, if the securities have produced large capital gains, it may be better to sell the securities before the 30-day deadline and repay the loan together with interest accrued up to the repayment date. The capital gain realized by your spouse is not attributable. Any income or capital gain your spouse makes by investing the capital gain amount will not be subject to the attribution rules, and you will then be in a position to make a new loan.

If the interest is not paid and the loan remains outstanding, income is attributed in all future years, even if the proper amount of interest is subsequently paid. It is possible that Revenue Canada would question a series of loans and repayments if it appeared that the spouse really intended to continue to hold on to the securities originally purchased.

TAX TIP **If the higher-income spouse gives or lends funds to the lower-income spouse, he or she will be in a better position to borrow on his or her own account and put the acquired assets up as collateral. The income earned on the assets purchased with the borrowed funds would not be attributable.**

Your spouse should have no trouble leveraging his or her investments using this technique, possibly two or three fold, if suitable assets are purchased with the borrowed funds. Remember that you cannot guarantee the loan; otherwise the attribution rules will apply to all the income earned by your spouse.

TAX TIP **If you are planning to take up residency in another country, transferring assets between spouses may result in tax savings when you file your last Canadian tax return. Remember that the attribution rules no longer apply when the transferring spouse becomes a non-resident. The options are many and they are complicated. Get professional advice as far in advance of leaving the country as possible. The attribution rules will apply once again, however, if you return to Canada.**

No Attribution of Business Income

If you give or lend funds to your spouse, and your spouse uses the funds to earn business income, as opposed to investment income or income from "property", the business income is not attributed to you. Almost any type of business income qualifies. You may want to glance at Chapter 9 on tax planning for the self-employed.

In 1988, however, the Government clamped down on situations in which one spouse would give or lend funds to the other to invest in a limited partnership. Such partnership income is generally considered to be business income and would not be caught by the attribution rules. However, the attribution rules will now catch limited partnership income and regular partnership income earned by the spouse, unless the spouse is actively engaged in the business activities of the partnership. The attribution rules would also apply to investment income of the partnership.

Chapter 9 explained several income-splitting ideas, including paying a reasonable salary to your spouse and children for work performed in the business, establishing a spousal partnership if both you and your spouse are involved directly in the business and ensuring that family members profit from the business's profits by owning assets that are rented to the business. If your business is incorporated, it may be possible for family members to own shares in the corporation. Profits then could be paid out to your spouse and children as dividends on the shares.

Attribution Rules and Corporations

Setting up a corporation to hold investments and involving your spouse or children in the ownership of the corporation will not help you side-step the attribution rules. These kinds of corporations, which essentially include those that earn primarily investment income or income from renting real estate, are not considered to earn business income. The attribution rules apply to them, but not to other small business corporations, which were defined earlier to be Canadian-controlled private corporations engaged in carrying on an active business primarily in Canada.

The corporate attribution rules apply to transfers of property or loans made to the corporation after October 27, 1986. Arrangements made before then are not caught. Generally, such corporations are set up as shells with the spouse and children owning a large number of the outstanding shares. The higher-income spouse then lends funds to the corporation or transfers his or her own investments to the corporation. Subsequently, all shareholders participate in the corporate earnings. Essentially, the corporate attribution rules say that if you make such a transfer or loan, and your spouse or children own 10% or more of any class of share and will benefit from the loan or transfer, you must receive a certain return annually in respect of the amount lent or transferred to the corporation. If you do not, and one of the main purposes behind the loan or transfer made by the higher-income spouse was to avoid or reduce tax, the attribution rules will apply.

These rules are complex. They apply in a variety of situations and cover indirect transfers. Make sure you get competent professional advice if you are contemplating setting up an investment holding company.

Income Splitting With Your Children

Loans to children who attain the age of eighteen in the year in question, loans to a common-law spouse and loans to related individuals other than children are among the loans that previously were not subject to the attribution rules. However, the attribution rules have been expanded to apply where an individual lends property, including money, to a non-arm's length individual and one of the main reasons for the loan is to reduce or avoid tax on income from the property or substituted property. The income earned by the borrower from the property or substituted property will be considered to be income of the lender and not income of the borrower. However, the rules will not attribute capital gains or income from a business. For the purposes of the attribution rules, a partner's share of income from a partnership will be considered to be income from property if the partner is a limited partner or a general partner who is not actively involved in the partnership's business or a similar business on a regular, continuous and substantial basis.

These new rules will not apply to loans that bear a commercial rate of interest, as long as the interest charged on the loan is, in fact, paid no later than 30 days after the year to which the interest relates. In addition, these rules do not apply to property that is transferred outright, that is, a sale or a gift.

The new rules will apply to loans outstanding after 1988. For loans made before 1989, the rules will not apply to income relating to any period ending before 1989.

Splitting income with your children produces larger tax savings than splitting income with your spouse. Your child can earn up to $2,500 (1988) before your tax credit for the child is affected. (Your spouse can earn only $500 before your married-status tax credit begins to decline.) And the combined federal and provincial tax credit for dependent children is only about $100 in 1988 ($200 for your third and subsequent children). The married-status tax credit is $850 in 1988.

Most parents arrange to split income with children to lower the cost of educating them. Is it worth it? Let's say that you are faced with paying $6,000 of your children's educational expenses, which do not include tuition that might generate a transferable tax credit (see Chapter 3). You are in the middle tax bracket, which means your marginal tax rate is 40%. To come up with that $6,000, you must earn $10,000, on which you will pay tax of $4,000 (40% of $10,000). If your children can earn that income and not pay a dime of tax, only $6,000 need be earned to finance $6,000 worth of education expenses. The worst that can happen is that you will lose a couple of hundred dollars in tax credits for your dependent children — a small price to pay for such an efficient way of generating these funds.

Bear in mind that sales or gifts of capital property to your children are considered to take place at fair market value, even if you receive no consideration from the child as a consequence of the sale. You must recognize any capital gain or loss at that time, although the gain is eligible for your lifetime $100,000 capital gains exemption.

Trusts and Income Splitting

One of the drawbacks of splitting income with children is the uncertainty of actually placing the ownership of assets in the hands of someone under the age eighteen (this is not to say that giving assets to children eighteen years of age or older is any more comforting). Theoretically, you lose control over the asset. This is not always a problem, but where it is, you might want to make use of a trust which has your children as beneficiaries.

You, as the settlor of the trust, give or lend money to the trust or transfer assets to it. Your children are the beneficiaries, which means they are entitled to the capital and/or earnings of the trust, according to the terms of the trust. You, and perhaps your spouse and another person would be the trustees, which means that you decide how the trusts funds are to be invested and how much and in what manner the earnings and/or capital of the trust is to be distributed. In other words, you have effectively transferred ownership of the assets to your children but you retain control over them. Note that if property transferred to the trust can revert to the settlor, if it can pass to persons determined by the settlor after the time the trust was created or if it cannot be disposed of except with the settlor's consent or direction, the attribution rules could apply.

The income earned by a trust is taxed at the top rate each year, unless it is distributed to beneficiaries. Such income does not lose its identity on distribution, so if Canadian dividends are distributed to your children, they will still be entitled to claim the dividend tax credit. If your children do not need the income in a particular year, you can elect for the income to be allocated to them for tax purposes (the preferred beneficiary election), but actually the amounts are left in the trust to earn more income. This is commonly done if the child is not taxable.

A trust must be set up properly if you are to accomplish your income-splitting goals; therefore it is imperative that you get legal help.

Techniques for Splitting Income With Your Children

First, you should note that a number of the techniques discussed above under income splitting with your spouse also apply to splitting income with your children. You may want to review the ideas to see if any apply to your particular situation.

TAX TIP Consider depositing all family allowance payments in a bank account in the name of the child. Income earned on these amounts is not attributed.

Revenue Canada considers these amounts to belong to the child if they are properly segregated. To retain control, open the account in the child's name "in trust", with you or your spouse as the "trustee". Even with a conservative investing policy, you might be able to accumulate up to $15,000 in the child's name by the time family allowance payments stop.

TAX TIP Since the attribution rules cease to apply in the year the child turns eighteen, you might consider buying deferred interest securities (GICs or term deposits) in the name of a child who is fifteen or older. The three-year accrual rules come into play if the child is younger than fifteen.

The amounts must, in effect, be given to the child. Previously, amounts were lent on an interest-free basis, and the child used the investment income for school expenses. Once he or she left school, the loan could be repaid. The new rules that apply to loans made to family members of any age curtail this type of planning, if one of the purposes of making the loan was to reduce or avoid tax on income generated by these funds.

When buying the deferred-interest securities, you might pick maturities that correspond to the dates the child needs the amounts for school expenses. In this way, you will have retained some control over the investing and distribution of the amounts, although the child will be able to dictate how the amounts are spent. A trust will solve this problem.

TAX TIP You might want to consider contributing to a Registered Education Savings Plan (RESP) for your children. The income earned in such a plan is sheltered from tax and amounts eventually paid to your children are taxable in their hands.

These plans come in several varieties. With most, you must contribute when the child is quite young. Large amounts can be contributed, and with at least one plan, you can decide how the amounts are to be invested. The catch with these plans is that income from invested amounts is only payable to the child if he or she attends college. The child is the only beneficiary under the plan. But with several plans, you can designate the amounts to be paid to almost anybody attending college, including yourself, if the child doesn't make it to college.

Only the interest earned on funds contributed is taxable. If amounts are not paid out to a student, you will receive only your capital contribution back from the plan, not any income earned on your contribution. Check the details of the various plans carefully and consider what other options are open to you—RESPs are not without their risks.

TAX TIP At some point before 1990, you might consider opening an RRSP for your young children and contributing up to $5,500, whether or not they have earned income for purposes of an RRSP. The income earned in the RRSP is tax sheltered and not attributed.

Tax is payable on the entire amount by the child when amounts are withdrawn from the RRSP, assuming that the child is at least age eighteen. However, if the child uses the RRSP to fund educational expenses, chances are that his or her income will be low enough not to attract any tax, even if amounts are withdrawn from the RRSP over several years. You may have to shop around a bit to find an RRSP issuer who will open a plan for your young children. This plan must be undertaken before 1990. After 1989, children under nineteen are not permitted to have an excess contribution in their RRSPs.

TAX TIP Since capital gains are not attributed, consider buying capital property in the names of your children. Mutual funds that produce little income and mostly capital gains are ideal, as is real estate.

Bear in mind that rental income is considered to be investment income in most circumstances and therefore is attributable. If you purchase rental real estate in the name of the child, it may be worthwhile mortgaging it to the hilt. Losses will be incurred in the first few years of ownership, but these will be attributed to you. Eventually rents will increase enough to offset these losses, but then CCA claims (depreciation), should keep rental income to a minimum for another few years. By that time, the property should have appreciated significantly in value and it may be time to sell.

If rental income is positive and being attributed, you might consider selling the first property and buying a second, more expensive one, once again in the name of the child. It would take several more years to generate positive rental income on the more expensive property, but your potential for larger capital gains would be increased.

TAX TIP **If you are in the business of farming, don't forget that you can transfer eligible farm property to your children and avoid recognizing any capital gain on the sale.**

You are permitted to designate any value from cost up to fair market value when you transfer eligible farm property to your child. The transferred value becomes the child's cost of the farm property. The definition of a child is quite broad, and includes grandchildren and great grandchildren. On such a transfer, you are also entitled to the lifetime $400,000 capital gains exemption as well as the general $100,000 exemption. Thus you would probably designate a value considerably above cost. No tax would be payable by you, and less tax would be payable by your child when the farm is eventually sold.

TAX TIP **Consider bequeathing amounts in trust to your grandchildren under your will, instead of to your children. The children would then act as trustees of the amounts. There would be no attribution because attribution ceases on your death, and the income would probably be taxed at a lower rate than if it were inherited directly by your children. Keep in mind, however, that**

testamentary and *inter vivos* trusts are generally deemed to have disposed of all capital properties at fair market value every 21 years.

This technique is only one of many that can be considered as you are designing your estate plan (see Chapter 15).

Splitting Income With Your Parents

With the double-digit inflation of the 1970s and 1980s, and the high cost of housing in many of our cities, it has become more and more common for children to augment the income of their retired parents, who even less than a decade ago thought that they would have enough to live on for the foreseeable future. In the past, the most common way to funnel income to a parent was to set up an interest-free loan. The parent would then invest it as he or she saw fit. The income was not attributable and would be received directly by the parent. This system had much to say for it, compared with giving amounts periodically to the parents.

Unfortunately the Government disagreed. Such loans may now be caught under the attribution rules, unless the loan is made on commercial terms and interest is charged at either commercial rates or the prescribed rate, and that interest is paid within 30 days after the end of the year. Only investment income is attributed – capital gains are not. However, you can still *give* amounts to your parents and avoid the attribution rules.

For the attribution rules to apply, one of the main reasons for making such a loan to parents must be to reduce or avoid tax on income generated by the funds that are lent. If you can establish that this was not a main reason for making the loan, the attribution rules should not apply. Unfortunately, the onus is on you to prove it, not on Revenue Canada to disprove it.

Several of the techniques for splitting income with your spouse also apply to splitting income with your parents. Some of these may be more palatable than writing out a cheque once a month.

TAX TIP **If your parents no longer own their own home, consider purchasing a condominium or similar home for their use. Any capital gain arising will not be taxable since your parents are entitled to their own principal residence designation (see Chapter 4).**

TAX TIP **If it is unlikely that each of your parents will be using up their respective lifetime $100,000 capital gains exemptions, you might consider transferring ownership of some assets to them. Choosing assets that also generate some income will help you supplement your parents' income.**

Transferring assets to your parents involves one major problem — how do you ensure that you will get your property back when your parents pass away? Most people would not wish their assets to be used by their parents and then distributed among several brothers and sisters. There is no elegant solution to this problem, other than ensuring your parents provide properly for you and your family in their wills. Using a trust to hold non-income producing assets would, however, be feasible. Your parents would enjoy the assets of the trust during their lifetime, and then the trust assets would go to you.

TAX TIP **If your parents are dependent on you for support, you may be entitled to claim the equivalent-to-married tax credit, which was $850 in 1988.**

You should bear in mind that by supplementing your parents' income directly, you might inhibit your access to the equivalent-to-married tax credit. More importantly, you may impair your parent's ability to claim certain provincial or federal income supplements available to the elderly. You should probably sit down with your parents and determine how large a transferred amount must be for it to be worthwhile giving up these sources of income.

14
Separation and Divorce

Chances are good that you have heard this complaint from someone who has just gone through a divorce: "I wish I had been given better advice!" This is not advice from friends, or legal advice from a divorce lawyer, but financial advice — particularly tax advice from a qualified professional. That's why more and more separated couples are going to court with both their divorce lawyer and their tax specialist. The savings they come up with often pays both their bills.

The tax rules that spell out the deductibility of alimony and maintenance payments, and the recipient's inclusion of them in income for tax purposes, have been redefined over the past few years to accommodate a great variety of divorce agreements. And a number of new provisions have been added to tax law to reflect changes in provincial family law that require a division of a variety of assets. In the past, the tax consequences of divvying up assets sometimes meant that Revenue Canada ended up with almost as much as the ex-spouses.

Recent changes in the family law of several provinces require the dividing up of business or corporate assets on the dissolution of a marriage. The tax implications of such asset divisions are beyond the scope of this book. In any case, you should be getting competent professional advice.

Tax planning around divorce is not a case of one spouse getting the better deal at the expense of the other. By taking advantage of a variety of opportunities and co-operating when it comes time to spell out obligations, both parties can end up better off. After all, if the taxman gets less, there ought to be more to go around.

Alimony and Maintenance

Alimony or maintenance payments made to your spouse are deductible for tax purposes, if they meet certain very specific conditions. Your spouse must include deductible payments made by you in his or her income. For convenience, we will use the term spouse, even though you may be divorced and remarried. For income tax purposes, "spouse" also includes a common-law spouse recognized under provincial family law.

For the payments to be deductible, three main conditions must, in general, be met:

- ☐ The payments must be made on a periodic basis for the maintenance of the spouse and/or children.
- ☐ The payments must generally be made pursuant to a decree or court order or judgement, or pursuant to a written agreement.
- ☐ The paying spouse must be living apart from the receiving spouse at the time payment is made and throughout the remainder of the calendar year.

Note that the payments must be made *periodically*; lump-sum payments do not qualify, even if made by instalment. Generally, the recipient must have complete discretion over how the payments are to be used, except in the case of third-party payments and payments singled out in the divorce or separation agreement to be devoted to a particular use. Generally, the amount of the payment must be specified, although indexed payments may qualify for a deduction, as may certain third-party payments of no specific amount. Indexed payments qualify if the formula for adjustment is an acceptable one, for example, payments adjusted in accordance with changes in the Consumer Price Index. On the other hand, amounts payable in accordance with variations in mortgage payments or by reference to a proportion of the payer's income will not qualify as an allowance.

Payments made before the date of a court order or written agreement are deductible if the payments are made in that year or the preceding year and the payments are mentioned in the order or agreement as having been made or received. Of course they will be included in the income of the recipient.

Third-party payments, such as mortgage payments made directly to the bank, educational expenses made directly to the institution or dental costs made directly to the dentist, are deductible, if the court order or separation agreement took effect after May 6, 1974. However, the order or agreement must specify that the payments are required to be made and they must be made on a "periodic" basis. As well, for more recent agreements, the court order or agreement must specify that the relevant provisions in the tax law apply to third party payments. This essentially protects the payer spouse who may eventually make third-party payments not foreseen in the court order or separation agreement, but which would otherwise be deductible.

Lump sums or payments of capital are not deductible. For example, settlements at the time of divorce cannot be claimed by the payer, and do not have to be included in the income of the recipient. There is one major exception, however. While the downpayment on a home to be occupied by the spouse would not be deductible, payments on account of principal and interest on the mortgage would be, up to 20% of the original amount of the debt in any one year. Bear in mind that the spouse would have to include this amount in income, but would not actually receive any cash from the spouse with which to satisfy any resulting tax liability.

TAX TIP If you have the cash available and your spouse is receptive to the idea, consider making a lump-sum settlement rather than periodic payments. However, this should only be done on the advice of an accountant who can provide reliable cash-flow projections that detail alternative financial positions for both you and your spouse.

While you will not receive a tax deduction for the lump-sum payment, both you and your spouse could be better off in the long run, depending on the numbers your accountant crunches out. Not to be ignored, and perhaps just as important as any tax savings, is the independence a lump-sum settlement provides for both spouses. The recipient is not dependent on an ex-spouse for support, but rather on his or her own ability to manage the lump-sum funds. And the payer spouse is freed from the burden of making regular payments, that while perhaps not a problem at the moment, could be in the future. Professional advice is a must.

TAX TIP If you have to take legal measures to enforce payment of alimony or maintenance, your legal costs are generally deductible for tax purposes. However, the legal costs associated with the separation and divorce are not deductible.

Legal costs to enforce payment of alimony or maintenance are only deductible if the payments sought must be included in the income of the recipient. Legal costs incurred in obtaining or enforcing a court order for a maintenance allowance, where the individual must sue the spouse or former spouse, are generally deductible also.

Attribution Rules on Separation and Divorce

As can be appreciated, the attribution rules could wreak havoc with any financial agreements made between spouses on separation or divorce. The attribution rules (see Chapter 13) essentially state that any income or capital gains earned by your spouse on assets transferred to him or her are attributed to you and must be reported in your income tax return. The rules prevent this income from being taxed at a low rate in your spouse's hands when it would have been taxed at a higher rate in your hands.

Upon separation or divorce, the attribution rules cease to apply. The spouses must be living apart as a result of the marriage breaking down. In this case, the spouses must jointly elect for capital gains not to be attributed after the date of the breakdown of the marriage. The reason for the election is to prevent one spouse from shouldering an unexpected tax liability. This could occur if a capital asset were sold for a sizeable gain, most of which accrued during the marriage.

Retirement Plans

Tax-free transfers of funds from one spouse's RRSP to the other's are allowed if the transfer is pursuant to a decree, court order or written agreement. Retirement-income payments eventually made will be taxed in the hands of the spouse who is the annuitant under the plan. As well, the special rules that prevent the transfer of funds from one spouse to another by means of spousal RRSP contributions (see Chapter 5) do not apply in the case of RRSP transfers on the breakdown of a marriage.

Special tax-free transfers are also allowed between registered pension plans, although it may be more common for the benefits from a plan to be split between the spouses. In this case, each spouse would receive the appropriate pension payments directly from the plan and be taxable on them.

It has also become common to split accrued Canada/Quebec Pension Plan benefits, and the eventual payments from the CPP/QPP, between estranged spouses. Each spouse is taxable on the amount each receives. You must have been legally married and living with your spouse for a minimum of 36 consecutive months.

Principal Residence

On the breakdown of a marriage, it is essential that the tax-free status of any accrued gain on the family home be maintained. Generally, if you and your spouse own only one home, there will not be a problem. For example, if your spouse continues to live in the home, he or she will be able to claim the principal residence designation on the sale of the home for each of the years it was occupied before and after the marriage.

Remember that a married couple may designate only one home after 1981. This one-home only rule applies in the year the marriage breaks down, providing you were living apart at the end of the year. In the following year, each of you are entitled to your own principal residence designation for a home.

The situation is more complex when two homes are owned. For example, if each home is sold several years after divorce, each spouse will want to claim the designation for the years during which they were married, but only one home may be claimed for those years after 1981. It is in the best interests of both spouses to maximize any exempt gain—the less Revenue Canada gets, the more the spouses get. They will also want to account in some manner for the portion of the future tax liability on the second home that arose during the years of the marriage. There are several solutions to the problem.

First, one spouse could forego his or her principal residence designation in favour of the other for the relevant years of the marriage. However, it may be more suitable to arrange for ownership of the houses to be transferred at the time of the marriage breakdown and use the available principal residence designations. The home with the largest accrued gain would be transferred at fair market value and any gain would be exempt under the principal residence rules. Ownership of the second property would be transferred, if necessary, at cost, so no immediate tax liability would result. Because of the "plus one" in the principal residence exemption formula (see Chapter 4), one year during the marriage may still remain exempt, which could be used to reduce the taxable portion of any gain that eventually arises on the sale of the second property.

Personal Tax Credits

In the year the marriage breaks down, you have a choice of either claiming the married status and dependants personal tax credits to which you normally would be entitled, or claiming your alimony or maintenance payments as a deduction. You cannot claim both. The spouse receiving the payments must include them in income, no matter which method the payer spouse chooses.

TAX TIP Before deciding whether to claim tax credits or deduct support payments, do the calculations both ways on your tax return. Remember that one is a tax credit and the other a deduction.

It is also possible for each spouse to claim a portion of the dependants tax credit, if they can agree on the specific amount. In this case, each must report an appropriate portion of family allowance payments in income. The spouse who receives the family allowance payment in the following January is entitled to claim the refundable child tax credit in the year the marriage breaks down.

If you are a single parent and supporting your children, you may be entitled to the equivalent-to-married tax credit for one of those children. This tax credit is a maximum of $850 (federal) in 1988, exactly the same as the married status tax credit. Any income earned by the child in excess of $500 reduces the amount of the credit. To be eligible to claim the credit, generally you must be living in a self-contained domestic establishment with the child. If you share the home with another person, only one equivalent-to-married tax credit is available for the home, even though there may be other qualified parents and children. The tax credit may be shared with another eligible person, if the two of you agree on the sharing arrangement. If you can't agree, neither of you may claim the credit.

15
Estate Planning

Estate planning is nothing more than ensuring that your family and heirs are taken care of in the way you want. Putting an effective estate plan into operation is another story, especially if your affairs are even a little bit complicated.

A great deal of financial and tax planning can also be included under the estate-planning banner. For example, retirement planning ensures that your family and other dependants are well taken care of after you retire, whether you are around to enjoy the fruits of your labours or not. Recently, much more emphasis has been placed on retirement planning because of longer life spans and a tendency toward earlier retirement. One of the goals of income splitting is to put assets into the hands of your children so that tax now and on your death is minimized or even eliminated.

From just these two examples, you can gather that there are three basic objectives at the heart of any estate plan:

- ☐ Ensure that your assets go where you want them to go on your death.
- ☐ Ensure that your dependants are provided for in the way you intend them to be.
- ☐ Minimize taxes and any other expenses that might eat away at your estate on death and leave less for your heirs.

Books have been written on estate planning. It's a complex topic that covers a variety of law, including tax law and provincial family law, that requires the participation of a variety of specialists and that offers literally hundreds of planning opportunities. It's also an area where professional advice is a must. And not just tax advice. At some point, you should be talking with a lawyer, your investment counsellor, an insurance specialist and perhaps even your family doctor and a real-estate agent. This chapter does nothing more than survey a few of the essentials of estate planning.

The Importance of an Up-To-Date Will

Dying intestate (without a will) is messy. It can defeat almost every bit of estate planning you have undertaken. Provincial law dictates how your assets are to be divided if you do not have a will.

Your will should be reviewed at least every five years by your lawyer and also by your tax adviser if your affairs have become at all complex. It should also be reviewed in light of changes in the law, particularly family law, which has recently been overhauled in Ontario. In some provinces, including Ontario, the law virtually dictates how "family" assets are to be divided even if you have drafted the most comprehensive will imaginable. And it should be reviewed if your personal circumstances have changed. For example, your will is invalid if you subsequently become divorced. Your will should also be reviewed if you get married, if you adopt a child, if one of your beneficiaries dies and even if you make a large, tax-free transfer to your RRSP.

Insurance

Having a proper insurance program satisfies a variety of goals. The most important one is to replace income lost on your death and to provide funding for the purchase of assets that you planned to acquire eventually. Insurance is also used extensively in business situations to buy out partners or partners' heirs. Some forms of insurance are looked on as investments.

There is simply no substitute for insurance in many situations. The death benefits from insurance are generally not taxable. Basic term insurance is cheap if you are relatively young, is very easy to acquire and is easy to understand. Other types of policies are more expensive, but they usually do more for you. Generally, the cost of permanent or whole life insurance remains level over the lifetime of the policy.

Taxes on Death

There are no actual death taxes in Canada. However, generally you are deemed to have disposed of your assets immediately prior to death, possibly giving rise to capital gains being realized. These would be recognized in your final income tax return. There is one major exception, however. All assets passing to your spouse or a spouse trust are transferred at cost; therefore, there are no immediate tax consequences. Assets passing to anybody else, including trusts, are generally subject to the deemed-disposition rules. As well, there are a variety of tax-planning measures that the professional advisers to your estate can undertake after your death to keep taxes to a minimum. Nevertheless, only so much can be done unless you have put your affairs in order during your lifetime.

The executors of your estate will be responsible for payment of any taxes owing in your final income tax return and for taxes payable on income earned on your assets before they are distributed to your heirs.

Having outlined how your estate is taxed on death, we also want to point out that, although tax saving is one of the objectives of estate planning, it is probably one of the least important. In fact, if saving taxes means, for example, that you must tie up your assets so that your heirs can't use them or even cannot be provided for properly, your whole estate plan could be undermined.

Estate Freezing

In many ways, estate freezing is simply an extension of income splitting. The idea behind this type of planning is to transfer any future growth in value of an asset (and hence any future tax liability) to your heirs, but ideally, you would retain control over the asset during your lifetime. This type of transaction freezes the value of the asset to you for tax purposes. However, it also can mean incurring an immediate tax liability, since you may have to recognize a capital gain when ownership of the asset passes to your heirs. Bear in mind, though, that the gain is eligible for your lifetime $100,000 capital gains exemption.

Often, estate freezes are conducted by means of a corporation, rather than through a direct sale or transfer, in which case tax may be minimized or even eliminated. Ownership of the shares in the corporation is structured so as to ensure that growth in the value of assets accrues to your heirs, while you retain control over the corporation, and hence over the assets, during your lifetime. Generally, personal assets can be transferred into a corporation with no tax consequences, since the corporation is considered to acquire the assets at your cost. Your estate-freezing objectives may also be attained by forming a separate "holding" or investment corporation. Obviously, this area is complex and demands professional attention.

Statutory Estate Planning Opportunities

How registered pension plan amounts are dealt with on your death depends to some extent on your particular plan, and on the pension-benefit options you have chosen. Pension reform requires that all pension benefits arising for years of service after 1986 provide for a pension to be continued to be paid to a spouse should the beneficiary of the plan die after retiring. As well, a spouse must be entitled to a lump-sum benefit from the plan if the beneficiary should die before retiring.

The RRSPs rules on death are different. Generally, if you have begun to receive a retirement income from your RRSP, your spouse may step into your shoes and become the beneficiary under the plan. If your RRSP has not yet matured, the entire amount may be transferred to your spouse's RRSP on a tax-free basis. Otherwise RRSP amounts are taxed in your final income tax return, with one exception. If you had no spouse at the time of death, amounts can go directly to your children or grandchildren, who must have been financially dependent on you. However, such amounts are limited to $5,000 times the number of years the child is under the age of 26. These amounts are taxed in the hands of the children. If a child is dependent by reason of physical or mental infirmity, there is no limit. These RRSP amounts may be transferred to the child's RRSP on a tax-free basis.

Tax law also provides for the protection of the principal residence exemption should you die. For these purposes, the surviving spouse is deemed to have owned the property throughout the period during which it was owned by the deceased.

The additional $400,000 capital gains exemption on the transfer of farm property and small business corporation shares was discussed in Chapter 11. This additional exemption is available, as well, to shelter capital gains realized as a result of the deemed disposition arising on death. In addition, when qualifying farm property is bequeathed to your children, grandchildren or great grandchildren, and certain criteria are met, it will be deemed to have been disposed of by the deceased and transferred to the beneficiaries at its adjusted cost base to the deceased. Accordingly, any gain or loss is deferred until the farm property is ultimately sold.

If capital property is bequeathed to a charity, the deceased's legal representative may designate an amount between cost and fair market value to be the proceeds of disposition and the amount of the gift for tax purposes. Ideally, any taxable capital gain will be minimized and the deduction for the charitable donation will be maximized.

The transfer of business assets, including shares of corporations, on death is complex and well beyond the scope of this book. A variety of estate-freezing and insurance techniques can ensure that your wishes are carried out exactly as you intend.

Reviewing Your Estate Plan

As can be appreciated, your estate plan must change with changes in your financial and personal life to remain effective. It should be reviewed periodically, perhaps as often as every year. Don't forget that external factors, such as changes in the law, can affect much of your planning. It will pay dividends in the long run for you to develop your estate plan with professional advice. The more you are familiar with how it works and how the pieces fit together, the better you will be positioned to let them know when changes might be necessary. Of course, you want an adviser who will let you know of regulatory changes that could affect your planning.

16
The Bottom Line

One of the easiest ways to save a few bucks during the tax season is to carefully observe the tax law's filing requirements. A variety of penalties and interest on unpaid taxes can mount up in a hurry if you are late filing your return or are late with your tax payments. Even a little bit of carelessness can cut an unpleasant swath through your pocketbook. If you have gone to the trouble of reading this book and have put a few of the tax-planning ideas into operation, there is no point in torpedoing your plans by ignoring a few of the basic rules.

Filing Your Return

As noted in Chapter 1, your return for a particular year must be filed by April 30 of the following year. The balance of any tax owing is payable at that time. Income from an unincorporated business or partnership is reported in your personal return. If that business or partnership has a non-calendar year-end, income there from must be included in your income for the calendar year in which the fiscal year of the business or partnership ends. Remember that if you owe tax but can't pay it, the late filing penalty will be avoided if you send off your return before the deadline.

You must include your social insurance number in your tax return as well as your spouse's, if you have lived together at any point during the year. You also must reveal your social insurance number to the promoter of a tax shelter in which you participate, a partnership of which you are a partner and to the promoter of certain other types of investments.

Revenue Canada reviews your return and sends you a notice of assessment, detailing your actual tax liability. At this time, you either receive a refund cheque, a request for an additional payment of tax or a confirmation of the tax you calculated on your return. However, Revenue Canada can change its mind and reassess you at any time over the next three years from the date of mailing the original assessment notice. There is no time limit for reassessments if you have willfully evaded tax, or misrepresented your tax position, whether through neglect or even carelessness.

Genuine mistakes are not attacked. The tax law is complicated. Not that many taxpayers send in perfect returns that they have prepared themselves, especially if their affairs are at all complex.

You should keep your tax records for at least three years, and preferably longer. If you operate a business, you must keep your tax and business records for at least six years, and then you still may have to seek Revenue Canada's permission to destroy them.

Amending Your Return

If you have made a mistake on your return or received additional information that requires your tax liability to be recalculated, by all means let the tax authorities know. But do not send in a corrected return. A letter explaining the problem is all that is necessary.

If you receive a notice of assessment and do not formally object to it within 90 days of its mailing date, you are technically bound by it. However, Revenue Canada will generally permit you to amend your return for errors or omissions up to three years after the date of mailing of your notice of assessment, the same time limit the Government has for reassessing your return. You should note that Revenue Canada will generally not entertain amended returns from prior years based on the results of a court case, nor if the taxpayer has a change of heart regarding optional deductions.

TAX TIP Consider filing your current year's return to reflect the results of a favourable court decision. If your claim is disallowed, you would then have to file a notice of objection (see below). In effect, this puts you in the position of being able to successfully make the claim if Revenue Canada eventually agrees with the court decision.

Paying Your Taxes

Payment of your year's taxes is due by April 30 of the following year, which is also when your tax return is due. If you don't pay the balance owing by this date, interest is charged (see below). Revenue Canada is somewhat accommodating if you are unable to pay your taxes by April 30. If you explain your situation, you can usually set up a payment schedule that won't be too onerous. Revenue Canada will accept post-dated cheques—within reason. Don't post-date them two or three years hence.

As you are well aware, tax is withheld from your paycheque if you are an employee. If you think your employer is withholding too much tax, fill out a new TD-1 form and give it to your employer. This form details certain deductions and tax credits to which you might be entitled.

TAX TIP In some circumstances, it is possible to have the taxes withheld by your employer reduced if you are making deductible payments, such as alimony or maintenance, large RRSP contributions or if you have large tax shelter deductions. You must go through the Source Deductions Section of your District Taxation Office

to get clearance for your employer to reduce tax withholdings.

If you have other sources of income besides employment, or if you are in business for yourself or are a member of a partnership, you may have to pay tax by instalments. Revenue Canada provides a booklet in which you can calculate the amount you should be paying. Instalment payments are due quarterly. Beginning in 1990, they must be paid by the middle of March, June, September and December, instead of by the end of these months.

The amount you pay in quarterly instalments is based on the lesser of your estimated tax liability for the current year and tax paid in the previous year. Generally, no instalments are required if your federal tax liability is less than $1,000.

TAX TIP **If you discover during the year that you are paying too much in instalments, perhaps because your current year's income is less than expected, reduce your instalments accordingly. There is no point in paying too much tax and getting a refund six or eight months later.**

Penalties, Interest and Other Things to Avoid

If you do manage to run afoul of the filing regulations or other pieces of the tax law, be prepared to open up your wallet, or even visit your friendly banker.

If you file your return late, even if it's postmarked a day after the April 30 deadline, you are subject to the late-filing penalty of 5% of the unpaid tax. If your return sits in a drawer for a few months, the penalty mounts up, at the rate of 1% of the unpaid tax for each month (to a maximum of twelve months) you fail to file the return after the deadline. If you fail to file a second time within a three-year period, the penalty doubles to 10% of the unpaid tax, plus 2% of the unpaid amount for each month (to a maximum of twenty months) your return is not filed. As well, you might be subject to fines of $1,000 to $25,000, or up to twelve months imprisonment, or both, if you are convicted of an offence under the Income Tax Act.

If all this isn't enough, you will be charged interest on late payments of tax – whether your final April 30 payment or tax instalments. The interest rate is the prescribed rate, which is based on short-term interest rates. It is set every three months. Interest is also payable on penalties that are assessed and not paid. Interest is computed on a daily basis and is compounded daily. If your instalment payments are large and you are neglecting to make them, an additional, severe penalty may apply to interest in excess of $1,000 owing on late instalments.

TAX TIP When you do get around to writing a cheque, make sure it doesn't bounce. This will add $10 to your bill payable to Revenue Canada, and of course your bank will hit you with a charge as well.

If you fail to complete all the information required of you on your return, you can be fined $100 for each instance. This includes failing to report your social insurance number in several situations. Penalties also apply if you fail to supply Revenue Canada with the information that they request.

The penalties listed above are only minor compared with what might befall you, should you decide to willfully evade tax, or you knowingly make false statements on your return or generally misrepresent your income or deductions. Large penalties are not uncommon if large amounts of tax are sought to be evaded. Jail terms are not unheard of.

Disagreeing With the Taxman

Not everyone will agree with how Revenue Canada treats their tax return when they receive their assessment notice.

Ours is a self-assessing system, so there is no reason why you shouldn't file on the most favourable basis. After all, if you don't give yourself the benefit of the doubt, no one else will. If you think that you have a legitimate complaint, contact your District Taxation Office and explain your case. It's sad to report, but the taxman is right much more often than the taxpayer. Chances are your disagreement will end after a few minutes of explanation and you'll sign the cheque for the extra tax owing.

However, some cases are not resolved in this manner. If you still disagree with your assessment, you must file a notice of objection with Revenue Canada within 90 days of the date your assessment notice was mailed out to you. This is the only way to keep your case open. Revenue Canada will review your return. If they change the amount of tax owing, you will receive a notice of reassessment. If they don't, generally you will receive notification that Revenue Canada is not changing its mind. If you continue to disagree, or you have not heard from Revenue Canada within 90 days of filing your notice of objection, you may then appeal to the courts. Interest on this unpaid tax continues to accrue during the time your appeal is in process unless you post acceptable security when you object to your assessment, or unless, of course, you actually pay the amount in dispute and wait for a possible refund.

Before this, you should be seeking professional advice to confirm your opinions, especially if the amount of tax at stake is large. You might save yourself the embarrassment of arguing a losing case before Revenue Canada officials, and you could also save yourself some money, since interest will be payable on any tax still owing. Remember that the onus is on you to prove that Revenue Canada's assessment of your tax return is incorrect. You are more or less presumed guilty and must establish your innocence.

If you appeal to the Tax Court of Canada and the amount in dispute is less than $7,000 (federal tax owing for one year and any related penalties), an informal appeal procedure is available. You may represent yourself, or have your lawyer or accountant or other agent represent you. The formal rules of the court are not strictly applied. This appeal process should take about six months. If the amount in dispute is over $7,000, general court rules apply. You can still represent yourself, but this is not advisable. You will be up against a gaggle of government tax lawyers, and the court will expect to hear arguments and evidence from you in the same manner it would hear it from a lawyer. Unless you are well-versed in the Income Tax Act, as well as legal procedure and jargon, you likely don't stand a chance.

In theory, an appeal can be made further up the ladder to the Federal Court of Appeal, and then even to the Supreme Court of Canada. The Supreme Court must grant leave to hear your appeal. Your professional advisor will let you know if you have a case, what your chances are and how expensive the whole procedure is likely to be.

Tax Audits

The chances are very good that the average taxpayer will never meet a Revenue Canada auditor face to face. There are close to 15-million taxpayers in the country and only enough auditors to review about 35,000 returns a year, including corporate returns.

This does not mean that your tax return will not be scrutinized. First, the computer reviews your return as best it can. This is quite effective for the majority of uncomplicated returns. Revenue Canada also conducts slightly more complex internal computer audits on hundreds of thousands of returns, sometimes on a random basis, but these rarely translate into personal audits.

Revenue Canada is "in the business" of collecting money. It costs around $1 to collect $100 of tax, which is actually quite efficient compared to many other countries. This same type of efficiency applies to audits. There is no point in conducting an extensive audit unless the extra revenue collected justifies the expense. In other words, if you have either "suspect" income or "suspect" deductions, you are more likely to attract an audit. The odds get better if the amount of tax at stake is substantial, at least several thousand dollars.

Included in the "suspect" category are persons who regularly claim a multitude of tax shelter deductions, those who earn substantial amounts of domestic and foreign investment income and those individuals who conduct the type of business that lends itself to large write-offs. Periodically, specific income groups are singled out for close scrutiny, which often leads to an audit. In the past, these have included commission sales persons, waiters, waitresses, taxi drivers and even artists.

The bottom line is that your affairs have to be complicated enough to provide some scope for abuse before you are likely to be audited. If you earn primarily employment income, have only a few deductions and earn only a small amount of investment income, you are unlikely to be audited, even though you may have close to a six-figure income.

If you are audited, don't worry—assuming you have nothing to worry about in the first place. The audit is more a nuisance than anything else. You will be asked to gather everything together you used to prepare your return and show up at a Revenue Canada office. You can bring your professional adviser with you; we definitely recommend this, particularly if they prepared your return. The auditor will go through your return, look at your supporting material, ask a few questions and, with luck, give you a clean bill of health.

However, Revenue Canada has become adept at picking out lucrative "suspects", to the point where 85% of audits result in reassessments. If you disagree with the results of the audit, you will have to go through the appeal procedure, which begins with filing a notice of objection.

17
Facts on File

One of the keys to sound tax planning is good organization. And the sooner you tackle your organizing chores, the better. Remember, all the careful tax planning you've done may count for naught if you can't produce the records and the facts that you need at tax-filing time.

Keep in mind too, that a tax adviser's main function is to help you make the most of the tax law, so you can save money. You don't want to waste your adviser's time—and your cash—sorting through slips of paper.

In the following pages, we've compiled a checklist of some of the records and information that you'll want to pull together before you or your tax-return preparer begins to work on your return. So get started. A tidy sum in tax savings might well be your reward.

Note that many tax-return preparers send their clients questionnaires or checklists asking for data for the current year. They also would like to see your last year's return, if they don't already have it on file. Definitely plan on using the questionnaire, as well as the checklist below. It may well jog your memory for deductions you might otherwise forget, and, if filled out completely, should cut down on the fees paid for preparation of your return.

Accounting for Your Income and Expenses

Prior Years' Tax Returns Your tax return preparer will

want to know the status of prior years' assessments and/or reassessments. Interest on any overpayment of last year's tax must be included in your income in the year of receipt. Changes that Revenue Canada made to prior years' returns may affect your current tax liability.

Employment Bring copies of all T-4 slips, as well as any other written documentation from your employer that you think might have an impact on your tax situation. For example, additional contributions to a pension plan or some car expenses or reimbursements may not show up on your T-4.

Pension Income Bring along all T4A slips, as well as information on foreign pensions. Only half of United States Social Security payments are taxable in Canada.

Interest and Dividends Bring all copies of T-5 slips that detail your investment income from conventional sources. Remember that you may not receive a T-5 if only a small amount of interest or dividends is earned, but you still must report the income.

Capital Gains and Losses Bring your broker's information slips, which will detail the purchase and sale price, plus the related costs and date of acquisition, for conventional transactions. If you sold property to your spouse at fair market value and must recognize a gain or loss, bring your supporting documentation.

Foreign Investment Income Bring whatever documentation you receive, as well as your own records. In particular, your tax return preparer will want to know how much foreign tax was withheld from the income so a foreign tax credit can be claimed.

Tax Shelters and Other Investments Again, bring all the financial documentation that you have received. In most cases, it should come on one information slip, but this may not be the case with private investments. Financial statements supporting an individual's claim for certain expenses (Canadian exploration or development expenses, for example) must be filed with the return. These statements are generally provided by the broker or even directly by the general partner. Traditionally, they do not arrive until close to April 30, and often after that date. Accordingly, you might want to make a few phone calls to ensure you get this important information on time.

Real Estate Rental Income Again, all your records of income and expenses are needed. You or your accountant will have to prepare a statement of income and loss. Your tax-return preparer will determine whether your expenditures are deductible expenses, or are capital in nature and must be added to the cost of the property, as well as the amount of depreciation you are entitled to claim on the property.

Self-employment or Partnership Income Generally, your tax-return preparer will also prepare your financial statements for your business in a manner that is suitable for tax purposes. You must submit a balance sheet and statement of income and expense with your tax return. If financial statements have already been prepared, for example, where you are a member of a partnership, your tax-return preparer will want to review them to ensure they are suitable for tax purposes.

Other Income You may be receiving income from a variety of sources for which you do not receive any kind of information slip. For example, alimony and maintenance received generally must be included in income (see Chapter 14). If you are in doubt about whether the amounts are taxable, total them up and explain their source to your preparer. Gifts, lottery and gambling winnings (unless you are in the business of gambling) and most insurance proceeds are not taxable.

RRSPs Bring the slip received from the issuer of the plan. Don't forget about contributions made for the previous year but not deducted. For example, you may have contributed $5,000 in January or February and then discovered that only $4,000 was deductible last year. The extra $1,000 is deductible for this year, even though you sent the receipt in with last year's tax return. Also don't forget information slips for special RRSP contributions and for transfers between qualifying plans.

Medical Expenses, Charitable Donations and Political Contributions Charitable and medical expenditures must be backed up with official receipts in almost all cases. Cancelled cheques are not acceptable proof for charitable donations. If you did not get a receipt, explain the situation to your preparer. You must have proper receipts to claim your medical expenses. Don't forget that a wide variety of expenses are deductible. Bring everything to the attention of your tax-return preparer.

Other Deductible Expenses The Canadian tax system is stingy compared with others—it just doesn't allow you to deduct very many expenses. But there are a few. Safe-deposit box fees are commonly overlooked by many. And don't forget union or association dues, child-care expenses, tuition fees, moving expenses, fees for the management or safe custody of investments, accounting fees for recording investment income and investment-counsel fees. Certain legal fees are also deductible, including those incurred to earn income from a business or investment, to object to income tax assessments, to enforce payment of alimony or maintenance that is included in income, to collect salary or wages owing and to enforce payment of amounts owing if you are wrongfully dismissed. Again, if you are in doubt, ask your tax-return preparer.

The Early Bird Catches the Worm

Why is it so important to gather together all this information? The answer is simple. The more organized your data, the easier it is for your tax adviser to save you tax dollars.

And keep in mind that the earlier you start your planning, the better the tax-saving opportunities. In fact, the best plan is to keep your records organized on an ongoing basis. You should plan on working with your tax adviser throughout the year to ensure optimum tax savings.

The bottom line: It's never too soon for you and your adviser to start developing tax-saving strategies for the current year.

Don't forget to stay in touch with your adviser as your personal and financial circumstances change—you may get married, sell your vacation home or make a killing in the stock market. As well, your employment or self-employed situation may have changed or you may have engaged in unusual transactions, any of which may require that you make instalments of tax throughout the year. Remember, you must invest your time today if you are to save tax dollars tomorrow.